TAROT
Spreads & Layouts

A User's Manual For
Beginning and Intermediate Readers

Jeanne Fiorini

4880 Lower Valley Road, Atglen, Pennsylvania 19310

Dedication

This book is dedicated to all the students and clients who come with open minds and hopeful hearts to the Tarot table.

Schiffer Books are available at special discounts for bulk purchases for sales promotions or premiums. Special editions, including personalized covers, corporate imprints, and excerpts can be created in large quantities for special needs. For more information contact the publisher:

Published by Schiffer Publishing Ltd.
4880 Lower Valley Road
Atglen, PA 19310
Phone: (610) 593-1777; Fax: (610) 593-2002
E-mail: Info@schifferbooks.com

For the largest selection of fine reference books on this and related subjects,
please visit our web site at **www.schifferbooks.com**
We are always looking for people to write books on new and related subjects.
If you have an idea for a book please contact us at the above address.

This book may be purchased from the publisher.
Include $5.00 for shipping.
Please try your bookstore first.
You may write for a free catalog.

In Europe, Schiffer books are distributed by
Bushwood Books
6 Marksbury Ave.
Kew Gardens
Surrey TW9 4JF England
Phone: 44 (0) 20 8392-8585; Fax: 44 (0) 20 8392-9876
E-mail: info@bushwoodbooks.co.uk
Website: www.bushwoodbooks.co.uk

Text and photos by author unless otherwise noted
Tarot card background © Alison Bowden. Courtesy of bigstockphoto.com.
All text and diagrams by author.

Copyright © 2010 Jeanne Fiorini

Library of Congress Control Number: 2010937140

Designed by Mark David Bowyer
Type set in UniversityRoman Bd BT / New Baskerville BT

ISBN: 978-0-7643-3629-4
Printed in the United States of America

Contents

Acknowledgments

This book had its inception at the 2009 Reader's Studio, an inspiring annual Tarot event hosted by Ruth Ann and Wald Amberstone, and so first thanks must go to them for their sincere and arduous efforts on behalf of the Tarot community. Much appreciation is extended to Dinah Roseberry for taking the initiative to seek out the TarotWorks website, and then taking the idea of a spreads and layouts book to Pete Schiffer. Gratitude to Janet McCaa who generously offered to review the initial contract and provide a reality check when it was required. Thanks to Sharon and Margo for their feedback on the initial drafts, and to Annie, Roz, and Kalli, good friends throughout all the ways we've explored what is real and true and meaningful. Love and appreciation goes to my dearest Kate, always a source of pride and joy, for our continuing relationship and for her support of this unconventional work. This book would still be in the ethers, however, if clients and students had not generously shared their stories through the Tarot cards for these many years. To be doing the work of expanding the personal and collective consciousness is a perfect example of the fact that the Universe has much bigger dreams for us than we alone can imagine.

Preface

If you've chosen this book, chances are you've already learned a bit about Tarot cards and want to know how to use them in a practical and personal way.

Anyone with even a passing interest in the subject soon comes to realize that the Tarot is a complicated, multi-layered, seventy-eight-piece system with a long and colorful history despite – or perhaps due – to its mysterious origins. For some folks, this alone is enough to discourage further learning. The notion of ever having a friendly relationship with the Tarot can become a dauntingly impossible task, causing those colorful and intriguing cards to be placed in the back of the closet, never again to see the light of day.

But don't lose heart just yet. Although the Tarot is mysterious and complex, this doesn't mean that useful ways of using the cards need to be equally complicated. This book is a straightforward approach to spreads and layouts, specifically designed to simplify Tarot readings for novice readers, those well-versed in the subject, and anyone in between.

Anyone willing to put in a modest amount of effort can reap the benefits of Tarot's wisdom. All it takes is an understanding of a few key principles, the acknowledgment of the voice of intuition, and the trial and error of learning which techniques are effective for you personally. My hope is that this book will deepen your relationship with the Tarot by making that process of exploration and discovery a little easier.

—Jeanne Fiorini

Introduction

The seventy-eight cards of a Tarot deck form a powerful and complex system which enables access to the information and insight that sits in the deepest parts of our awareness. At its core, the Tarot is a tool for the development (and thus the expansion) of both the personal and collective consciousness. As with any other tool, use of the Tarot requires a bit of hands-on training in order to be effective in the task it was designed to accomplish. No worries: By using a simplified, demystified approach to spreads and layouts, and by keeping a few guidelines in mind, you'll soon be well on your way to developing a satisfying and enlightening relationship with your cards.

Here's something important to remember about Tarot spreads and layouts: There is no big mystery, no magical or arcane formula that qualifies them as authentic. Of course, there are the established and venerated layouts such as the Celtic Cross or the Gypsy spread, but these are complex, web-like patterns consisting of numerous cards with intertwining connections, and as such aren't always the best choice.

These particular layouts are not always the best choice, not because they are for "experts only," but because they provide much more input than is required. All those images and all those card meanings and all that information can be overwhelming, and in truth, are unnecessary. The good news is that Tarot spreads don't have to be complex in order to be effective. Let's face it, the seventy-eight cards themselves are challenging enough without adding a complicated layout to the mix.

A Tarot layout is, in its simplest terms, a statement of intention. By placing cards in predetermined positions, the querent is purposefully assigning a specific role to each of the pieces of their puzzle, allowing the position in the layout to establish a context for the meaning of each card. The action is much like being a director in the theater, choosing parts for your actors and subsequently pointing them to their marks on the stage.

For instance, while using a particular spread one might state aloud, "By placing this card here I'm asking for guidance in my relationship" or "The card in this position will represent a potential block to my success" or "The card which appears here will show something I may be avoiding." You'll find that by focusing intention clearly and methodically, very useful insights can arise from very basic layouts.

Throughout this book we will be looking at all kinds of queries: those dealing with money, relationships, matters of personal growth, issues of time and timing, dilemmas of choice and opportunity. We'll zero in on some very specific lines of questioning as well as be addressing some of life's big mysteries. We'll see that it doesn't matter whether the question is big or small: When you use a layout that is well-suited to the issue at hand, information will present itself through the cards much more readily than you may have thought possible.

Some layouts are better suited for certain types of questions than others, and we'll see that the line of questioning determines the spread, not the other way around. In acknowledgement of this, chapters herein will be defined by type of query so that access to an effective method for your line of questioning can be readily found and tested. The insights you gain through your exploration of the Tarot may be monumental; the methods you use to realize them needn't be.

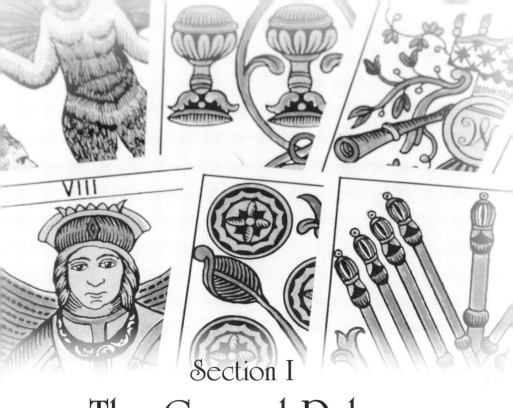

Section I
The Ground Rules

The Art of the Question

The Importance of Intention

Formulating a clear and concise question is the very first thing to do before working with your Tarot cards. In this preliminary but essential process, the impact of your personal intention cannot be overestimated: Intention is the key ingredient to the success of any reading. We're not talking about the "being a good person" kind of intention, but a "focusing of the mind" intention, the purposeful use of one's will. It matters not if you're reading for yourself, for a friend, or as a paid practitioner; the biggest obstacle to a reading of clarity and insight is lack of intention.

> **Important:** A clear intention serves to focus attention on the question at hand, not on the answer we hope to receive.

The Tarot is not about wish-fulfillment, but the pursuit of information, knowledge, and awareness. We use the Tarot to provide information, to help fill in the gaps in our knowledge as we search for answers: answers to a query, answers to our confusion, answers from spirit, answers to our discomfort, answers to our prayers.

It's very easy to reach for one's Tarot cards in moments of uncertainty, and begin pulling cards randomly from the pack. You might soon find yourself feeling even more uncertain, frustrated, muttering, "But what does this mean? What are these cards trying to tell me? Maybe I'll draw just a few more…Oh, I give up, I don't get it!" Of course you don't get it; you haven't asked a clear question.

The next time you reach for your Tarot cards, begin at the beginning. Start any session with your cards by first asking yourself, "Why did I pick up my cards today? What exactly do I need from them? What am I trying to learn or discern? What is the core concern or dilemma?" Be as clear as you can in your own mind about what might be the essential question at hand, peeling away the layers of questions until you get to the basic issue.

> **Important:** When setting your intention before using the cards, ask yourself: "What is it I really need to know?"

Consider the following scenario: Let's say you're feeling uncertain about the current state of a relationship. You might have been wondering, "Where is this relationship is going?" Although this is a fair question, if you go deeper you may find another thought: "Why is this relationship making me feel uncertain?" Looking even deeper you may find the question, "What needs are not getting met in this relationship?" This thought may lead to, "How can I take care of my needs within this relationship?" In a few short moments we've gone from "Where are we going?" to "How do I take care of myself?" These are very different questions with very different intentions.

Here's an example from an actual reading, illustrating the impact of a clearly stated intention: It was July, and a woman in one of our monthly Tarot reading groups had recently put her house on the market. In our attempt to be clear about our question to the cards, we came up with, "When will Vicki have a signed contract for the sale of her house?" We thought we were being very thorough by not asking the more open-ended questions such as, "What is going on with the sale of the house?" or "Will someone be interested in buying the house?" or even the simpler," Will the house sell?" Through our investigation of the cards on the table that night, we concluded that October would be the month in which she was likely to get a signed contract for the property. In the next month's meeting (August) we posed the same question to the Tarot and arrived at the same conclusion: October.

Vicki came to the October meeting with an odd smirk on her face. "The cards were right!" she declared. "I did have a signed contract in my hand in the first week of October. A couple came in with a cash offer and we had a deal. However, due to the suddenly-sliding stock market, the buyers wiggled out on a technicality and now I'm back to square one."

Oh, we were so close! The Tarot didn't let us down, nor were we incorrect in our interpretation of their message. But we had failed to be as concise as humanly possible with our query, not to mention the fact that the plunge in the stock markets was a wild-card element which came as a surprise to many people. This is a lesson to us all to think very carefully about what it is we really need to know, what is possible to know, and what we'd like the cards to address.

Since the literal phrasing of the question is so crucial, let's consider some of the factors above and beyond intention which come into play as we approach the Tarot.

Beliefs Inform the Question

The art of Tarot reading begins with the framing of a clear and concise question. This is our first task. But once we begin to be mindful and intentional about what we are asking of the Tarot, it doesn't take long before we find ourselves bumping into unconsciously held thoughts and perceptions.

If you want to know when you'll meet the man of your dreams, you have to first ask yourself, "Do I actually believe that such a person exists in this world for me?" If you are wondering if you and your sister will ever reconcile, you have to first consider your part in the relationship and what it is that you want from it in the future. If you're unsure about taking that job in Seattle, is it because you think there is an intrinsically "correct" choice and that you're doomed to a path of failure unless you choose IT and it alone?

Hey, how did the posing of a simple question get so tricky? Blame it on the paradoxically complex yet limited framework of our perceptions. We all hold unnamed thought patterns and belief systems in our unconscious minds, going merrily about our business until something happens which calls them into question. The beauty of the often-painful process of expanding one's awareness is that we're brought face-to-face with a previously unseen aspect of ourselves. Although looking directly into the mirror can be difficult, it gives us the opportunity to examine things more closely and make deliberate choices regarding which of these aspects to retain, reframe, or discard.

The Tarot is a marvelous tool for the unhinging of such unconscious material, and for unearthing the wisdom that is held in the recesses of our understanding. All sorts of information and enlightenment is available to us, if only we were to shine the light of our consciousness in its direction! And that is, in fact, what we do each time we open our Tarot deck: Shine the direct light of conscious awareness onto the pool of life's possibilities.

If we're going to look to the Tarot for such a service of enlightenment, we have a responsibility to approach the line of questioning with an equal accountability. The following posits have no right or wrong responses, but considering them may help you become more aware of the mind-sets and world views you bring to the Tarot reading process:

Are people ruled by destiny or free will?

Does God exist? If so, does He/She/It have an input/opinion regarding what we do?

To what degree, if at all, do you believe that spirit intervenes in life?

To what degree, if at all, are outcomes predetermined and/or unavoidable?

Is there a correct answer to any given problem?

Why are we on this earth?

What are the most important things in people's lives?

Do you think that people are intrinsically good hearted?

Is there Evil in the world?

Where does the information in a reading come from?

Why do people do what they do?

Is your basic personality that of an optimist? ...a pessimist? ...a realist?

> **Important:** Become as aware as possible of your ingrained perceptions and beliefs, since these factors influence not only your query, but any and all interpretations of what the Tarot puts on the table.

As an example, let's say the posited question is "How do I best achieve harmony with my family?" and the card drawn is JUSTICE. A person who believes that we each have a prescribed destiny to fulfill while here on earth might say something like, "Family harmony will be the natural result of doing what is right and honorable." Someone who believes that we are a product of our own free will might respond with, "You have a responsibility to speak up and speak out so that others who are less strong can be supported. Harmony might have to come as a result of conflict." A person with the voice of a realist might say, "It is what it is, and not much will change the family dynamics here. Accepting things as they are will be the best path to harmony."

> **Important:** There are no right or wrong interpretations here, simply an assortment of differing responses emerging from various world views.

What Are You Looking For?

Keeping an eye on the workings of one's conscious and unconscious beliefs is a good step toward an effective reading, so let's go back to the idea of "What is it I really need to know?" and look at ways to be even more precise in our questioning. Let's say a person has concerns about work. Which of these, if any, is the real issue?

What can I do to enhance the security and stability of the job I now have?

How can I be happier in my job?

How can I get along better with my coworkers?

Is it in my best interest to look for different work?

How can I make more money at my job?

How can I get a work schedule that fits better with the other responsibilities in my life?

How can I discover work that will feed my soul?

Is this a good year for me to retire?

Firstly, we cannot expect one vague question to address all of these specific points. Additionally, a person may have needed to pose several of these questions or others not here mentioned, and we cannot expect any one question, no matter how perfectly presented, to address all issues related to the query. Lastly, we need to recognize that the phrasing of each different query will foster a different response from the cards.

> **Important:** Your stated intention not only provides the framework for the cards you select on any given question, it also informs how you'll interpret those very cards.

For instance, drawing the THREE OF WANDS for the first question might encourage someone to look at the long-term prospects of their current job and be proactive in setting work-related goals; drawing the same THREE OF WANDS in response to the last question might imply that, indeed, the time to move along has arrived.

Don't Save it for a Rainy Day

Given the abundance of information that the Tarot is capable of conveying to our conscious minds, it's a shame that most of us call upon our cards only in times of distress. In much the same way that we call the doctor (only) when we have an ache or a pain, we seek out the Tarot when our hearts and minds are aching, with hopes of finding comfort and guidance within the images there. When a job is on the line, when a break-up is imminent, when health issues threaten a family, when life throws us lemons, this is when most of us reach for our Tarot cards.

> **Reminder:** The Tarot is available for all of life's matters, and should not be set aside until life is difficult or painful.

Just as it's true that by using preventative measures and by regularly practicing healthy habits one is ahead of the curve of physical wellness, any kind of ongoing interaction with your cards will give you not only a boost of self-awareness but also enhances confidence in the Tarot as a dependable source of insight.

There are innumerable happy and positive issues for which the Tarot can provide guidance:

- Perhaps you've landed a new job and are eager to make the most of the opportunity.
- A new relationship has come into your life and you'd like to see it develop in mutually beneficial and happy ways.
- Whether in good health or in recovery from accident or illness, you may be looking for ways to strengthen and maintain healthy well-being.
- A person might seek guidance about how to achieve a deepened sense of spirituality in everyday life.
- Parents might wonder how to best guide and support a teenage child.

What a waste it is to pack away the cards in a sock drawer, pulling them out only for emergency sessions! The Tarot needn't become a tool used exclusively in crisis management. Use the cards as a resource for conscious living regardless of whether lemons or lemonade are on the table.

Size Doesn't Matter

What about "big questions" vs. "small questions?" Is the issue of whether or not to buy the red car or the blue car a less valuable query than the one about how to discover my soul's work? The short answer here is "no."

We all have practical matters with which we need to contend. We all have spiritual aspects that await our discovery. Our existence here on earth is a mysterious blend of many layers of consciousness, and the Tarot is here to help us through it all. If an issue impacts your life, it is open to investigation and clarification through the Tarot. One simply needs to remember that the parameters that are useful in a decision regarding a choice of automobile are the same as those concerning a musing on the meaning of life: Be clear about your intention, streamline the query, create a concise question!

Important: If it matters to you, you can ask it of the Tarot.

No-No's

Yes, if it matters to you, you can ask it of the Tarot. If it is about you; if it impacts you; if it concerns you. It is not okay, however, to do what I call "looking in someone else's underwear drawer." You know, taking action on that insidious little tendency we all have to be curious about what other people are doing.

Number One

Here's the first no-no of Tarot reading: addressing queries regarding people and issues which don't directly involve or impact you. Questions such as "How is my ex-husband's new marriage going?" or "Is my daughter's best friend gay?" or "How much money does my neighbor make?" are clearly out of bounds. A good rule of thumb is to refrain from posing a question over the Tarot table that you wouldn't bring up in mixed company at a barbeque. In general, stay away from any query that is intrusive, none of your business, or just plain bad manners.

Important: Keep clear boundaries and mind your manners.

Number Two

The second no-no involves the use of the words "should" and "will" within the query itself. "Should I marry Sandra?" or "Should I make the weekend trip to see my parents" or "Should I take that job in San Jose" all imply that there is a correct answer written somewhere and that you'd darned well better discover it before you make a grave mistake.

Questions such as "Will I be happy if I move to Canada?" or "Will I find a life partner?" or "Will I buy a new house?" all make the assumption that the future is not in our control and is, rather, the result of forces beyond our knowing and our volition. For better or for worse, the pattern of a life is not that simple nor is it written in stone; no query should give power to the notion that it is either.

> **Important:** Phrase your query to reflect the fact that you have creative control over your life.

Number Three

No-no number three: delving into the 5- or 10- or 20-year plan. There are too many threads in the fabric of life's unfolding to give much credence to prognostications that go beyond the time frame of a year or two. This no-no also covers the scenario "If I were to move to Canada and if I married Sandra, then would I be able to buy a new house and be happy?"

> **Important:** Too many "ifs" spoil the question; don't go there.

Number Four

A final no-no, for your own peace of mind: Use a bit of common sense when posing questions to the Tarot, and don't ask questions to which you really don't want an answer, or to which no answer ought to be had. This involves the inevitable wonderings such as "When (or How) will I die?" or "Will my child ever come to any harm?" or "Will Joe and I be married forever?" These kinds of thoughts are worries in search of a guarantee, and not even the Tarot can provide us that.

Who is Right and What is True

The Tarot is a remarkable resource for information, insight, confirmation, support, and guidance. As you gain experience with the images, symbols, and card meanings, you'll find that a familiarity with a card meanings as well as an increased level of intuitive knowing is at your disposal. (Both one's intellectual and intuitive muscles are developed through an exploration of the Tarot.) Beyond an initial uncertainty of "What does this QUEEN represent?" and "to which element do SWORDS correspond?" you may find yourself pondering some tougher questions:

Are the cards always right?
How do I know if I'm getting correct information from the cards?

What if the cards say something that I don't believe?

What if the cards say something I don't want to hear?

Must I take what is on the table as the ultimate in truth and wisdom?

If the cards have clearly stated an advised course of action, does this mean there is an obligation to follow through on that advice?

What part do my own thoughts and desires play into interpretations, especially if my perceptions differ from the information on the table?

These are important ideas to ponder, and you will need use of the aforementioned intellect and intuition to arrive at answers that work for you. Our human hopes, fears, emotions, thoughts, needs, and desires are part and parcel of our interpretation of the Tarot, there is no getting around that. In fact, it is these very qualities which make the Tarot a vibrant and dynamic tool for the development of consciousness. But we need to remember that the Tarot is in service to us, not the other way around.

> **Important:** The Tarot acts as an informant to our awareness, not as the director of it.

The reading process is here to enhance and elaborate upon what we can know, not to tell us what to think or how to be. As readers and students of the Tarot, we are responsible for sifting through the information, sorting the useful from the superfluous, the accurate from the inexact, the real from the imagined, the true from the merely hoped-for. Never let any information that comes from the Tarot (or anywhere else):

- talk you out of your own good sense,
- dispel your own intuitive knowing,
- diminish your innate awareness of what is true,
- disengage your responsibility for any thought or action,
- lessen your sense of personal power.

What if Nobody Answers When
You Knock on the Door?

Even with a clear intention, heightened awareness, and all of your Tarot skills and knowledge at the ready, sometimes the cards just don't seem to provide an answer. It's not that we didn't get the answer we wanted and now we're grumpy, but that sometimes we run into a case where there is nothing discernible whatsoever on the table. The mind goes blank, the words run out, *poof* ... There's nothing to see, nothing to say.

This unsettling event signals that, for whatever reason, it's time to put the cards away. Maybe you've had enough for one session. Maybe your questions were headed in the wrong direction. Maybe whatever makes the Tarot "work" decided you were finished for the day. Or maybe there simply was no answer to your query. Period.

> **Important:** Sometimes there is no answer.

How can this be, that there is no answer? It could be that the timing or the query is off, or an issue is not yet resolved on any level, and hence no information regarding it can be imparted. When we hit a dead zone in a reading, the phrase "It is not yet written" often comes to mind. (In other words, things are still in the works, somewhere out there in the universe.) Lastly, we must remember that some questions are best left unanswered.

This is a hard thing for modern, thinking people to comprehend: that not all things are ours to know. Not all questions have answers, and not all that is knowable is available to us in any given moment. Our rational mind does not like this, but it's true. The best we can do is to knock on the door, question in hand, and hope that the Tarot will greet us with help and guidance.

unanswered
prayer

Reading Skills
& Other Practical Matters

The Tarot reading process is creative, exciting, and unpredictable. "Reading Skills and Other Practical Matters" is intended to provide concrete information about how to get the most from your Tarot readings, regardless of the spread, layout, or method used. All you really need in order to have a wonderful relationship with your cards is already inside of you; the information here is meant to guide and inform the journey, to shine a light on potential twists and turns along the way, and enhance confidence in your own unique Tarot adventure.

Using Your Intuition

Did you notice that the title of this section is "Using Your Intuition" and not "How to Tell if you Have Intuition" or "Tarot Reading for the Intuitively-Impaired?" Despite our obliviousness to it or a lack of confidence in it, we've all been given the gift of intuition.

Intuition comes to us in tandem with our more-tangible senses as part of the human guidance and orientation system. While it is virtually automatic for us to become acclimated to our physical senses, the effective use of one's intuitive sense requires the development of a particular skill: the recognition of intuition's often-subtle signals. Intuition shows up for different people in different ways, and thus it is useful to become familiar with how it shows up for you specifically. As the wise Tarot reader and teacher Geraldine Amaral points out, intuition development begins with asking, "How do you know that you know?" Gaining confidence with "how you know" will take practice, but the rewards are boundless.

> **Important:** We all have intuition; effective use of it takes practice and self-awareness.

For some individuals, intuition is a gut feeling with no causal factors involved: "I don't want to buy this particular house" or "I know that June and I will be friends for a long time." Other people experience physical sensations along with their intuitions: "Every time I go into that store I get a headache" or "When I spend time with Fred and Nancy I feel warm all over."

The entire body is, in fact, an excellent mirror for our intuitive knowing: Do your neck and shoulders physically tighten up (as if offering protection) around certain people? Does your throat go dry when you're about to speak aloud something which is untrue? Does your tummy do a flip when someone acts inappropriately in your company? Do goose bumps appear when something beyond rationale occurs? Indeed, intuition can be a full-body experience!

There are those folks for whom, when intuition speaks, literal words or phrases are heard in the mind: "That red car is a good one for you to buy" or "Stay away from Mr. Peebles." (We've all had that "little voice in the head" go off every once in a while, haven't we?) Sometimes the intuitive voice speaks in mental pictures: "Every time I look at my son's soccer coach I see him dressed in a Civil War uniform" or "My neighbor always has a dark cloud hanging over his head."

And then there is just plain knowing. When you know. Even though you don't know how you know, you just know. Simple as that. Once you begin to pay attention, all these phenomena are much more common than you might have previously realized.

Think of how much time and energy could be saved if we all acknowledged each bit of intuitive wisdom that inner guidance provided! And then again, think how easy it is (and how often it happens) that we either dismiss, disregard, deny, or otherwise talk ourselves out of what is communicated to our conscious mind from this nebulous place within us.

In daily life in general and in working with the Tarot in particular, the recognition, and then the nurturance, of one's intuition is an area where the paradoxically complex yet limited framework of our perceptions needs to be carefully monitored. In other words, we must consider carefully that which we would call a true intuitive "hit."

The teasing apart of actual intuitive information from the other material that is constantly flitting through our mind (fears, desires, plans, flights of fancy, wonderings, etc.) is at the core of intuition development. It takes time, practice, trial and error, and persistent self-examination to keep those wiggly thoughts and perceptions in line with what is true and real. But once you're clear about how intuition works within you, the task of filtering fact from fiction becomes much easier.

One more important comment regarding intuition: If you're not going to bring yours to the Tarot table, you might as well let a computer do the job of reading the cards. That's not a criticism, simply a comment on the nature of the Tarot reading process. There are boatloads of Tarot manuals and guidebooks and websites, all of which have the seventy-eight cards of the deck defined, delineated, sorted, and available for public use. There are no secrets here.

The secret—and the mystery—and the fun begins when intuition comes to the plate to offer wisdom and insight aside from what the guide-books can provide. It is intuition that can move Tarot reading into an art form. It is what makes a reading personal, relevant, and significant. Be sure to set a place for intuition at your Tarot table.

The Significator

You'll find the word "significator" in many Tarot handbooks along with the description of certain layouts and spreads. "The significator" is a somewhat archaic term associated with the more predictive aspects of the Tarot, but it does have a place in the simple layouts you'll find herein. What is a significator and what do you do with it?

> **Important:** The significator is a card deliberately and intentionally drawn from the deck prior to laying out the cards, and is selected to represent the querent, a person around whom the reading revolves, or the energy of a particular event or situation.

The significator becomes the center point of the layout, the focal lens for all the other cards that might be used in the reading. It is deliberately pulled from the deck before the layout begins, with ensuing cards being drawn in relationship to it. This process serves to call direct attention to a specific person or concept.

Examples: If you're doing a reading for a clear-minded and independent friend, you might use the QUEEN OF SWORDS as the significator. If the query involves her teenage son, the KNIGHT OF WANDS might be chosen. If you're looking at the possibility of major changes in the coming year, the WHEEL card could be helpful. If you're trying to understand ways by which to bring partnership into your life, THE LOVERS would be a useful significator.

You'll find a specific method with which to use a significator in the following pages, and there are simple ways to utilize this concept as you use your cards in other ways as well. But be aware: by taking a card out of the deck before laying out the cards, you've taken one piece from the seventy-eight-card deck, a piece which now cannot be part of your "solution." With a significator already on the table, you're not going to be playing with a full deck. (I love a good Tarot pun!) This isn't necessarily a problem, but something of which to be aware if you chose to utilize a significator in your readings.

Reversals

Cards that appear in a layout in a reversed (upside-down) position are a very common stumbling block and can become unnecessarily problematic. When reversed cards come into a layout, you have four possible options:

1. Disregard the reversed aspect completely. It's a perfectly acceptable choice to read the card just as you would have, had it appeared upright. There are those folks who believe that if you were meant to receive the "opposite" message for the reading, you would have received a different card entirely.

2. Interpret the reversed card to imply the opposite of what it might have meant, had it come in an upright position. For instance, pulling the Two of Swords upright could connote "peace of mind," whereas the same card reversed might indicate "anxiety."

3. Consider a reversal as an indication that the message of the card is blocked, hindered, resisted, or otherwise not accessed. Taking again the Two of Swords and using this method, one might say that peace of mind would be possible by making a few mental adjustments, or that peace of mind is coming soon and to use patience in the meantime.

4. Use any single one or combination of the above methods in whatever way feels useful and appropriate in the given moment. (Ah, creative control! It's one of the benefits of working with a system based on intuition.)

Once you've had some practice and experience with what works best for you, your interpretation style might develop into "Sometimes I read reversals, sometimes it doesn't seem to matter. I might try to re-position a card in the upright position, and if that somehow doesn't seem right, I'll leave it reversed and interpret it from that standpoint. It varies from reading to reading."

Reversed cards needn't become the bane of your existence. Actually, some pretty cool things can occur when cards appear "on their head."

- Do two personality cards face one another in a way they would not have, had they come in an upright position?
- Does the MAGICIAN, for instance, aim his wand at a particular card of significance when he's upturned?
- Do those agonizing blades in the THREE OF SWORDS fall away when this card is reversed?
- Does the HANGED MAN have a few more options for action in the reversed position than when he's upright?
- Does a card in a reversed position to the reader appear upright, and therefore more direct, to a querent across the table?

> **Important:** A reversed position provides alternative ways to view a card in relationship to the other cards within the layout, and thus offers additional avenues of interpretation.

The subject of reversals is one more area of learning that will benefit from your personal efforts of trial and error, where you will eventually find the method of usage that is best suited to you and your reading style.

What You Don't Get

We pay a lot of attention to the cards that show up in a reading. There's lots of pondering, listening, intuiting, and eventually the articulation of the just-right words in an attempted description of any given scenario. Of course, all that is good cause for doing a reading in the first place. But it's often important and just as informative to consider what *hasn't* shown up in a reading.

A fairly typical example is the situation in which a person wants to know more about a financial issue, and yet no PENTACLE cards appear. You might keep trying, however, pulling card after card, only to find that you couldn't buy a PENTACLE if your life depended upon the sight of it. Frustrating, yes; but here's the good news:

> **Important:** Cards that don't appear in a reading are neither part of the problem nor part of the solution.

While it's very convenient when the cards that show up in response to a query have the same tone and implication as the query, this hand-in-glove scenario isn't always the case. All of life's experiences are intertwined in complicated ways which are not always within our immediate zone of comprehension. It is only natural that the Tarot reflects these complex interconnections, and that we would see an overlapping of various suits (i.e., areas of concern) within queries.

Let's say you want to know how to best foster the relationship with your adult child, and draw three cards to point the way: TEN OF SWORDS, KING OF PENTACLES, and the WHEEL OF FORTUNE. We might have expected to find CUPS appearing in regard to a relationship query, but here we're dealt something much different.

These three cards suggest that this relationship is best fostered on your part (at this time) by a deliberate "stand by and lend practical guidance and support" posture (KING OF PENTACLES). While changes are in the wind for your child (WHEEL OF FORTUNE), he/she is likely to need very little from you beyond some pragmatic advice; and one might add, advice given only when requested (TEN OF SWORDS). Apparently, feelings and emotions (the realm of CUPS) are "not part of the problem or part of the solution" regarding the current state of this relationship. This does not suggest that one become detached from the child or change the way of connecting with them in any way. Rather, it tells you that what you have established emotionally is in working order, and now there are other areas where the child may need guidance.

> **Remember:** Absence of an element in a reading tells us, "If it isn't broken, don't try to fix it."

It's All Relative

When a green piece of paper is placed next to a red piece of paper, we are not surprised to observe an intensification of both hues and to notice that a distinct boundary appears between the two colors. If we were to place that same green paper next to a blue piece of paper we might experience a very different feeling of ease and harmony between the separate elements. Yet surprisingly, we would not be unsettled to realize that our perception of the green paper had shifted and was, in fact, dependent upon how it was seen in relationship to the adjacent paper.

This exact principle regarding the relativity of perception applies to each of the seventy-eight cards within the Tarot system. From the very moment it is pulled from the deck, a card shifts its identity from being a part of "the whole" into having a specific significance within the context of a query.

We cannot expect that, once we've learned specific card meanings, that those accepted interpretations remain forever inert, unaffected by time, experience, and the interplay with other cards. Given the fluidity of a card's meaning, here are three useful principles that guide accurate interpretation of the Tarot:

1. Good readers learn how to "notice what they notice" in any given reading.

The art of Tarot requires the ability to be responsive to what shows up in the cards. Don't confuse a familiarity with card meanings ("book smarts") to imply that a card's significance will remain static over time. Any image within a card can speak louder than usual on any given day in any given scenario, if the query warrants extra attention being paid there.

Let's say the TEN OF PENTACLES appears in a layout. The reader's eyes might be led to the couple in the middle ground of the card, perhaps speaking to the ideals of partnership, harmony, or marriage. The PENTACLES themselves might seem especially yellow in another scenario, drawing attention to the financial aspects of the situation. One might notice the solid tower in the background of the card, implying that, at least for the time being, all is well. Attention to animals depicted on the card might imply the use of instincts or the manner in which the forces of nature impact the query.

Notice what you notice; it's likely to be relevant to the question at hand. Allow yourself the time and space to let the images on the table communicate with you. That's why you're both there, isn't it?

2. Any and all cards need to be considered in context. All things are relative to all other things within any spread or layout.

Readers need to be sensitive to the subtle changes in card meanings that occur as a result of the presence other cards within the layout. For example, how might the SIX OF CUPS next to the ACE OF SWORDS have a different interpretation from the SIX OF CUPS next to THE SUN card? Or how does the KING OF WANDS change his attitude depending on proximity to the KING OF PENTACLES versus the HANGED MAN card? There aren't enough words to cover all the possible permutations!

Relativity remains an issue with single card draws, since with this method any one card is selected in response to a particular question and must be interpreted in relationship to that particular query. For example, does not the FOUR OF PENTACLES in response to "What can help me maintain financial security?" imply something very different than if it was drawn in response to "What prevents me from attaining financial security?"

3. One of the results of relativity within the Tarot is the fact that any one card can mean different things in different contexts.

For instance, we can imagine that the FOUR OF WANDS may mean "happy marriage" in one person's Past/Present/Future layout, and "the satisfactory sale of a house" for a different person using the same layout. How can we know the difference? This phenomenon can be very confusing for the novice reader, but it needn't be a deal breaker.

The critical requirements for an effective reading are a clear intention, a concise question, and use of the simplest spread that will get the job done. Remember to be clear about the motivation for and the phrasing of any query. Having done this, as long as the reader holds both a basic knowledge of card meanings and intuition at the ready, the rest will take care of itself.

Ready to Begin a Reading

You're ready to try out a new spread. You've got your Tarot cards, a quiet moment to yourself, and have chosen a layout. Now what? How does a person select the cards that will go into the positions of the template? There are a surprising number of options at your disposal! *Note that as we begin each of these methods, the cards are placed face down on the table.*

1. Shuffle the cards thoroughly, and then stack them all into one uniform pile. Drawing from the top, place one card after another, in order, into the positions of the layout.

2. Mix all the cards together by moving them around on the table, schmooshing (that's a technical term) them together with your hands in a circular pattern. Choose cards at random from this unorganized pile, filling the positions of the layout either in order or as directed by intuition as to where they fit in the layout.

3. Shuffle; then set the cards into one uniform pile. Cut the deck into as many piles as there are positions in the template. Draw the top (or the bottom) card from each pile and place it in its assigned position within the template.

4. Put all the cards into a uniform pile and cut the deck once, separately and in order, for every position in the layout, selecting either the card at the bottom of the top portion or the card at the top of the bottom portion for each position.

5. Devise you own method of getting the cards into the layout. (Creative control strikes again.)

Important: The key ingredient required with any method of selecting cards is intention. Know what you're doing and why you're doing it.

Say to yourself, silently or aloud, statements such as "What appears in this position will help bring a positive relationship into my life" or "This card will represent a potential hindrance to my success." Give yourself a moment or two, allowing the intention to settle and to quiet your mind, before drawing your card.

Note: Once you begin choosing cards, it's a good idea to leave all the cards in the face down position until all cards within the layout have been selected. This helps keep intention clarified, and prevents the cards that have already appeared on the table from becoming a distraction.

Expandability

The spreads and layouts in this book are the templates for your readings, the structures through which your questions may be answered. You may find that your concerns are fully addressed through the use of any one of them, but you will no doubt confront situations where only parts of your wonderings are satisfied by what appears in a spread. Additionally, it is not unusual that one well-answered query will lead to another question … and another. Not to worry, spreads and layouts are expandable.

What you will find on the following pages are the starting points for your query, not the final word. Give yourself permission to build on the templates provided here. These layouts are simple and effective ways to use your cards, but that doesn't mean you can't add a card here and there for clarification and/or expansion of an idea. As long as you deliberately state your intention for any position beyond what is contained within the template, you're clear to take off in your own direction.

> **Important:** You have creative control over with how your reading progresses, as long as you remain deliberate about the intention and purpose for all cards within the layout.

The Turkey Spread: It's Not a Holiday Condiment

One autumn several years ago, the students in one of my monthly groups came into class to find that their activity for the evening was working with the "Turkey Spread." Having run out of ideas gleaned from books and other resources, I'd designed a layout in the shape of a Thanksgiving turkey: The bird's beak represented "where I am going," its head connoted "where my mind is," the body was "what I've established," and each of the feathers represented an "ability or attribute that can help me be successful." The whole thing was very silly, but here's the point: The concept of building your own layout can be a creative and useful notion.

> **Important:** Not only are spreads and layouts expandable, they are able to be formulated into any shape or design which you can imagine.

Any shape or design you can imagine! As previously stated in the "Introduction," there is no big mystery, no magical or arcane formula that qualifies spreads as authentic and real. This means you can make up your own spread, or use any shape or form with which you are familiar as a basis for a card layout. This idea can lead to some very interesting possibilities.

Let's say you're well-versed in the principles of Feng Shui. You may want to use the Ba Gua map to check out the energy in your home or office "Tarot-style," by placing a card in each of the eight sections of this octagonal map. If you're a yoga practitioner, perhaps you'd enjoy using the outline of your favorite yoga pose to survey the energy of your physical body by placing cards at key points or junctures. An astrology aficionado could spend hours with the wheel of the zodiac (or someone's astrological chart) and a Tarot deck, analyzing the relationships between the cards and astrological houses, planets, and aspects. You get the idea. And by now, you can likely guess the most important factor in the creation of any and all custom-made layouts. You've got it: Intention.

Once you know what you're doing, why you're doing it, and what you hope to accomplish, just about anything goes.

Start With the Big Picture

As you experiment with the spreads and layouts provided herein, give yourself a moment after selecting the cards and before literal interpretation begins, to take in the generalized sense of the reading as a whole. Allow the cards within the reading to speak to you with their pictures and their colors and their essence before you begin to discern their meaning.

Give attention to how this unique group of cards makes you feel. Is the group before you peaceful? Chaotic? Sad? Energetic? It's often true that the whole is greater than the sum of its parts, that the message of the reading in its entirety may not be discernible in any one particular card on the table. The gathering of the overall sense of the reading will provide a container within which your intuition can expand as the reading progresses.

> **Important:** Start with a landscape view of a reading, then zero in on the details.

Train yourself to catch an eagle-eye view of the scene before focusing in on individual cards and their specific meanings. Even as you begin to intellectually discern a reading's message, remain with general themes as you proceed: Which images really catch your attention? Is there a consistent tone to the cards you see? Is there a plethora of a certain suit or MAJOR ARCANA cards? Is any one particular suit, element, color, or image markedly absent from the reading? Any and all initial observations are priceless as you move more deeply into a reading's message.

Sometimes, having observed the big picture will let you know that the answer on the table is bigger than the question which was posed. While you might have asked about your current work situation, you could be looking at a reading that informs you of an outworn belief that no longer serves you...or about choices you had perhaps not yet considered...or about a relevant area of your life that was not part of the initial inquiry, but which has import nonetheless.

The Tarot has a way of giving us not only what we are ready and able to absorb, but of what we need to become aware. Your questions may seem minor, but don't expect the cards to always respond in like manner.

Beyond the Books

Book knowledge can and will be useful to a student of the Tarot. Card meanings, connections with astrology and kaballah, relationships to the four elements, numerological significances – whew, there's a lot to learn about the Tarot! The material found in books is, however, only the framework upon which the relationship with your deck will be built. What happens beyond the absorption of that information, after the basic foundation of Tarot information has been set?

We could think about the next step in familiarizing yourself with the Tarot in the same way as you would the challenge of learning to play the piano. Although some people will take to it easily and others will have to work with a more earnest focus, we all are capable of attaining some degree of mastery with the task.

The eighty-eight keys of the piano can be likened to the seventy-eight cards of the Tarot: These are the elemental components with which we will work. Each piano key, as with each card, is a separate and unique entity, yet is intimately connected to the whole and is a critical part of the system. No one key on the board is any more important than another. The same is true of the seventy-eight pieces of the Tarot, regardless of how we might feel about any one particular image.

We begin learning to play the piano by learning the notes and the scales; with the Tarot we study card meanings and the significance of symbols. Our study leads us to the memorization of simple melodies (layouts) and the testing of new skills (intuition development). And then we practice.

Maybe the time comes that we're confident enough in our abilities to play a piece of music for our friends and family (read for others). And like the pianist who moves us as their heart and soul flow through the music, so will readings be enhanced and brought to life by intuition and our own uniquely-personal interpretation of the cards, regardless of the level of expertise.

As we develop proficiency, appreciation for and connection with our instrument expands and our options become more varied and interesting. Sometimes we might feel like playing a classical piece, another day it might be jazz. It's all music, and if we've learned our foundational skills well, we can go anywhere we like.

This book is intended to help you play jazz with your Tarot deck. It has been constructed as a primer of simple, "classic" methods of reading cards. It is meant as a bridge between a basic knowledge of card meanings and the ability to have a facile, open, effective, and enjoyable relationship with the Tarot.

The classics will always hold their place of relevance and meaning, as will methods of improvisation and invention. It all takes practice, but regardless of the implemented technique, important things begin to happen when the wisdom of the Tarot is accessed. They happen because the Tarot is, essentially and intrinsically, a tool for the evolution and expansion of consciousness.

It's About Consciousness

It's no small thing to embark upon the road of learning the Tarot. It is not that it is difficult, but it is never-ending. The exploration of the Tarot is a journey with countless avenues into other systems of thought, resulting in rabbit-hole after rabbit-hole of inquiry and discovery. But the beauty of it is that you can go as quick or as slow or as far or as deep as you like, the Tarot will respond to your attention with insight and wisdom regardless of the pace of your efforts.

This fact, and the related intricacy of these many and winding paths reflect the golden nugget of truth about the Tarot: that it is a system with taproots into not only the personal consciousness of the querent, but the querent's personal unconscious and the collective unconscious of all humanity.

The Tarot is a symbolic system that works in, on, and with the same material as the dream world, the trance state, the birthplace of myth and archetype. To open the book of Tarot signifies a willingness to meld minds with an alternate plane of consciousness in order to bring something new into awareness. Reading the Tarot is about empathy with forces beyond our understanding, compassion for all life's experiences, honoring the voice of intuition, and participating in something unseen. It's about moving out of one's immediate, known sense of self into something wider and deeper.

We use the Tarot as we seek guidance, insight, comfort, and meaning in our daily lives, and well we should. But that action, although it is likely motivated by personal concerns, does not occur within a vacuum. When you touch a piece of truth by means of the Tarot, it affects not only your own conscious awareness, but that of the group as a whole. You add to the pot, so to speak, of what has already been established within the "stone soup" of our collective knowing.

> **Important:** When you work with your Tarot cards, you become a participant in the shaping and shifting of human consciousness.

Quantum science is beginning to prove something that we've known instinctively all along: that we're all connected, that we share a common energy field, that the ripple effect of our thoughts and actions is far greater than we could have dreamed. In this light, it is not an overstatement to say that the consciousness of the human family is impacted each time someone uses their Tarot deck in an effort to seek out that which is true and real.

So while it remains important to recognize that the Tarot is a wondrous tool by which to be guided through life's successes and challenges, let us not forget that our personal concerns connect us to a greater purpose: a widening scope of global consciousness and an expanded vision of what is possible for us all.

It is exciting, hopeful, and full of responsibility to remember that as we each walk our own unique path of self-development, we simultaneously participate in the group process of consciousness evolution. May the spreads and layouts herein provide a framework to support your journey along this path.

Section II

Simple and Effective
Spreads & Layouts

Template Introduction

The following spreads and layouts are designed as templates for particular lines of questioning. You will find the chapters organized by the nature of the query, allowing easy access to the key spread for any particular topic. Included with each layout (with the exception of the one-card draws) you will find suggestions as to how to expand the basic pattern, for those times when you have the need or desire to do so.

Although these templates are presented as patterns for specific types of queries, it is perfectly acceptable to use any one of them for whatever line of questioning you choose. Also, be reminded that you can amend and build on these foundational layouts in the ways which suit your personal preferences – and your intuition – as readings unfold.

Important: In any and all layouts illustrated herein, remember to ask yourself: Does intuition provide any insight beyond the meanings of the images and the surface definition of the cards?

Give it to Me Straight
1-Card Draw

While it's true that a lot of information can come from a single card, it's also true that very few questions can be thoroughly addressed by one card alone. We're likely to get a piece of the puzzle with one card, but not the whole picture. Most dilemmas in life are multi-faceted and complex, putting a lot of pressure on a single card to clarify the entire scene. However, for the rare moments when a piece of essential, no-nonsense guidance is called for, a one-card draw can be a valid option.

Important: Keep a one-card query simple and to the point.

Here are some suggested lines of questioning for one-card draws. You'll see that each question addresses a distinct aspect of the issue at hand:

What could be my guiding principle in this situation?

Which action serves my best interest at this point in time?

What is the most effective way for me to reach a positive resolution of this situation?

Which aspect of my personality helps me move forward in a positive manner?

Which aspect of my personality might be blocking me?

Of what must I be aware in order to be successful?

What is essential to my well-being at this time in my life?

At the present time, to what must I pay attention?

What can I learn from this particular experience?

What do I need to know or remember as I move through this experience?

What is in my highest good at the present moment?

What is trying to emerge in my life at the present time?

How do I best stay centered and true to myself?

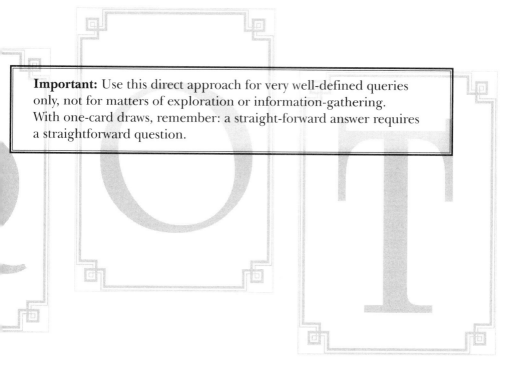

Important: Use this direct approach for very well-defined queries only, not for matters of exploration or information-gathering. With one-card draws, remember: a straight-forward answer requires a straightforward question.

Card for the Day
1-Card Draw

The Tarot is an effective tool for crisis management, is useful in moments of self-reflection, and is a wonderful avenue for intellectual stimulation and existential ponderings. But let's not disregard the Tarot's ability to guide us through life on a day-to-day basis! With ongoing use, a personal relationship to and deepened understanding of the images and meanings of the cards will be developed.

An easy method for accessing this deepened relationship with your cards (and therefore with yourself) is to develop the practice of drawing a "Card for the Day."

The purpose of this exercise is to be informed and guided by the "Card of the Day," but precisely how and in what area of your life this takes place is up to you. It is a good idea to write down or make journal entries regarding your "Card of the Day," noting any overall patterns which may occur, as well as your personal reflections on the cards selected.

At the beginning of your day, before things get too hectic and your time becomes occupied with a multitude of thoughts and responsibilities, take a moment to calm your mind, being open to whatever thoughts and feelings arise. When ready, take your cards, articulate a statement of intention that suits the tenor and activities of your life on that particular day, and draw one card from the deck. When stating your daily intention, use uncomplicated phrasing such as (but not limited to):

Of what need I be mindful today?

How do I best support myself today?

To what must I give attention today?

What could be a guiding principle for the day?

What is the best attitude to bring to interactions with others today?

What strengths and abilities do I bring to the situations of the day?

How do I serve the greater good during this day?

What can help me move through the day with peace and grace?

Of what need I be wary today?

What can help me be successful today?

What can help me be happy today?

How can I bring happiness to others today?

What might be the lesson or challenge of this day?

By spending a few moments with the selected card (the images, impressions, and your interpretation of it), the mind will be set in motion to recall that card during the day. At the end of the day, revisit the card and its message to you. Pay attention (making journal entries if you wish) to the ways that the meaning of the card – in its varied and possibly disparate aspects – had relevance during your day. By keeping track of the cards drawn over a period of time, you have the opportunity to reflect back upon ideas which, on any particular day, may have been confusing or unclear.

Use concepts such as these as you muse on the daily card and its significance:

Where did the card's meaning show itself today?

In what ways did the card's message help me?

Of whom/what did the card make me aware? Did the card's message affect my interactions with others?

Did the card's message surprise me during the day?

Did the card's message confuse me during the day?

Did I apply the card's message in a way that changed my approach to anything or anyone?

Did the card's significance shift or alter itself during the course of the day?

Were there instances of different aspects of the card appearing at different parts of the day?

What part of the card's guidance was particularly useful?

Important: If and when you begin to establish this ritual as part of your day, draw only one card on each day. Over time you may wish to draw up to three cards, but it's wise to start with a single card per day at the start.

Helper/Hindrance

2-Card Layout

When we find ourselves in a muddle, it can be very difficult to understand what we feel and what we want. Self-awareness and confidence tend to fly out the window in times of stress and confusion, whether we're challenged by work life, love life, or any other issue. To make matters worse, it's very common for different elements within us to have opposing wants and needs. (You know, the adult needs the whole grain but the kid wants the sugar.) Pretty soon we don't know whether we're coming or going. Help!

By using the following method, a simple but intentional selection of two cards, you will be able to discern specific aspects, actions, attitudes, or ideas that could be helpful as you work toward the resolution of a particular problem, and to those factors that might be hindering that same effort. It's useful to look at these two aspects as a pair, comparing and contrasting the cards appearing in each position.

Here's a place where the reader will need to look at both their strengths and their foibles with equal honesty and compassion. The directions for this method are simple: Being very clear about which card is being drawn for which position, choose one card for each side of the issue. (Sample question: What can help me find a well-paying, satisfying job, and what might be hindering that same effort?)

Diagram #1

Card #1

What might be helpful in the development or resolution of the issue

Card #2

What might be hindering the development or resolution of the issue

> **Important:** The positioning of either card to the left or the right is arbitrary. What is important is that you are clear in your intention as to which card is a helper and which is a hindrance.

Imagine – and beware of – the erroneous "insight" that can occur if the positions within the template are confused or reversed! Remember to keep your intention clear as you choose cards for their positions within the layout. You need to know what you're doing and why.

When using the "Helper and Hindrance" method, you'll be faced with a pair of cards that have a relationship to one another, defined by aspects such as:

How are these two cards similar?

How are these two cards different from one another?

Is there anything (an image, an element, a person, a quality) that is consistent in each card?

Does something (an image, an element, a person, a quality) appear in one card as part of the solution and also in the other card as a part of the problem?

Is there a very clear distinction between Card #1 and Card #2?

Do you have to split hairs to find differences between Card #1 and Card #2?

Do reversed cards appear? If so, what does the reversed position depict or imply?

Does either card show an aspect of which you are presently aware?

Does either card show you something new that needs to be considered?

You'll find that there is much information to be had by an intentional draw of only two cards!

Guidelines for Expansion of the Layout

The "Helper and Hindrance" method cuts straight to the point of this exercise, and as such, is best used when kept simple and direct. However, should you decide to expand on the initial information received from the cards on the table, here are a few suggestions:

Draw an additional card to help augment the trait that appears in the helper position.

Draw an additional card to help soften or release the hindering force.

Draw an additional card to show how to bring the Helper and the Hindrance into harmony.

Draw an additional card to show an alternative means of resolving the issue.

General Overview with Past/Present/Future Spread

3-Card Layout

Sometimes we want to take a look at the big picture, getting an overview of life as it is unfolding. "What have I accomplished?" "What am I doing" and "Where am I going?" You may recognize these questions as those we often ask ourselves, in many different scenarios and for many different reasons. These types of general inquiries can be easily addressed by the use of this three-card layout.

While focusing on the significance of each of the positions separately, draw a single card for each position within the layout:

Diagram #2

Card #1: The recent past/What I have experienced in some area(s) of my life

Card #2: The present situation/What I am currently experiencing in some area(s) of my life

Card #3: The immediate future/What experiences may lie ahead in some area(s) of my life

The "Past-Present-Future" layout is an excellent framework for obtaining a birds-eye-view of the recent evolution of life's events. It can confirm what we think and feel; it can clarify issues, dispel our doubts, and can provide visual images for the path we've been traveling. It is best used as a measure of the recent past (the three to six months prior) and the immediate future (the three to six months which lie ahead).

Now is a good time to talk about the idea of what is meant in these layouts by "the future." Consider what appears in the future position as "the likely evolution of the current energies and dynamics as they continue to unfold" rather than "that which is coming no matter what." The future is a fluid concept, affected by countless variables, not the least of which is our own free will.

Important: Any layout will be more effective in describing the immediate future than a long-term scenario, since variables coming into play over time can dramatically change the course of events. The fact that longer periods of time enable more variables to come into the picture makes a defined future very difficult to discern.

More to the point of using the Tarot as a tool for conscious and intentional living, it's important to make the best of the present moment and allow the future to become what it will. Without getting too metaphysical about time, space, and the nature of reality, we need to remember that we are always in the present moment and that "the future" is a subjective and pliable reality which never really arrives. Let the Tarot help you make the best of your "now" so that your "later" can be as much of your own making as possible.

As you look at the overview which the "Past-Present-Future" layout affords, here are some thoughts to help discern the message:

What is the general tone of the three cards on the table?

Does anything appear to be stagnant or stuck in place?

Are there places where things are moving quickly?

Where – if at all – does energy, strength, or power appear?

How does this combination of cards make you feel?

Do we see an unfolding story in these cards?

Is there any particular card or image that catches your attention? If so, what might that indicate?

Is there any one card that seems to have more strength or power than the others?

Where is there conflict – or harmony – among the images on the cards?

Is there any continuity or commonality that appears amidst these three cards?

Do reversed cards appear? If so, what does the reversed position depict or imply?

Do common themes, suits, or symbols appear, and what might that imply?

Where, if at all, do MAJOR ARCANA cards appear and what does this tell you?

If Personality cards are present, are they indicative of particular people, aspects of yourself, or both?

Is something new coming into the picture?

Do the cards point to a specific issue or a broader view of events?

Guidelines for Expansion of the Layout

Although this layout is very effective in describing the experience of a querent, "information gaps" are likely to exist: What might yet be unresolved from the past? What remains to be established in the present? What might be needed as the future unfolds?

With the "Past-Present-Future" layout, we have a pattern especially well-suited for expansion through related lines of questioning. Here are some guidelines for building upon this most basic spread:

If there are unresolved matters from the past, draw an additional card or two (placing them between Card #1 and Card #2) to provide further information or to help with closure.

Draw an additional card or two (placing them either above or below Card #2) to help clarify questions about the present situation.

Draw a card or two (placing them between Card #2 and Card #3) as helpers or guides for moving forward in a positive manner.

Draw an additional card or two (placing them after Card #3) for more information about what you might expect as the future unfolds.

If the cards of the future seem worrisome, select a few additional cards with the thought "What, if anything, can I do to amend this outlook?" or "How can I best deal with this outcome should it occur?"

If the cards of your future look pleasing, select a few extra cards for "How might I bring this experience to its greatest fulfillment?"

Since the matter of time and timing is so very tricky, you will find a layout method specifically designed to work with issues of timing on page 81.

General Overview with Body/Mind/Spirit Spread
3-Card Layout

This application of a three-card layout offers an opportunity to view the current state of our three-fold nature: as a body, a mind, and a spiritual being. Our physical, mental, and spiritual aspects are intimately entwined with one another; this layout allows us to see how these three different aspects impact one another.

While focusing on the significance of each of the positions separately, draw a single card for each position within the layout:

Diagram #3

Card #1: The current state of the body

Card #2: The current state of the mind

Card #3: The current state of the spirit

The order of the cards within the layout is arbitrary, as is the fact that they are shown here placed in a horizontal line. Use whatever pattern and order of placement feels right for you, intuitively. Keep it simple, beginning with three cards only, using your intention to define the placements.

Consider these thoughts as you view your Body-Mind-Spirit combination:

Where, if at all, do cards of strength and power appear?

Where, if at all, do cards of frailty, caution, or fear appear?

Is one of the aspects more intact than the others?

Is one aspect noticeably weaker than the others?

Is any one aspect calling out for attention?

Do you see a harmony-or a schism- among the aspects?

Is there a common theme among the three cards shown?

Are differing needs expressed by different aspects?

What sorts of interplay do you see between these aspects and the elements of the Tarot? (For instance, does a PENTACLE – material world – card appear in the Body position? Or is a SWORD – thoughts and perceptions – card appearing as a component of the Spirit? Conversely, does a PENTACLE appear in the Spirit position? Or does a SWORD card appear as an indicator of the Body?)

What might it imply that certain elements appear as indicators of certain aspects?

Do reversed cards appear? If so, what does the reversed position depict or imply?

Where, if at all, do MAJOR ARCANA cards appear, and what do they indicate to you?

Guidelines for
Expansion of the Layout

If you'd like additional information beyond the initial three cards that have been drawn, the following methods can help expand the boundaries of this layout:

Draw an additional card to provide reinforcement or support to any aspect.

Draw a card in response to a query such as "What does my spiritual life need in order to flourish?" or "How can I sustain and support my physical being?" or "What does my mental life need in order to be clear and calm?"

Draw a card in response to a query such as "What might be preventing my spiritual life from flourishing?" or "What might be hindering my efforts to provide greater financial security" or "What obstacles exist in establishing a calm and clear state of mind?"

If there is a problem area within your initial three cards, draw a card or two to help resolve the issue seen there.

Draw a card (or two) to help guide the integration or harmonizing of these three different aspects.

Draw a single card as an indicator of how to put forth your best effort toward overall well being.

General Overview with Three Sectors of the Tarot
3-Card Layout

The seventy-eight cards of the Tarot can be divided into three main sectors: The MINOR ARCANA, the MAJOR ARCANA, and as a sub-division of the Minor series, the Personality Cards.

The numbers "1" through "10" of each suit within the MINOR ARCANA address the "nuts and bolts" of daily living. The particulars of our experience will show up here: the tasks at hand, what is accomplished, the state of emotions, how and what is observed and perceived, the challenges, the difficulties, the blessings. These 40 cards illustrate what we have to work with in all the layers of our earthly manifestation, be it our emotional, physical, mental, creative, spiritual, monetary, or intellectual reality.

The MAJOR ARCANA cards depict the larger-than-life, archetypal energies which impact our lives, whether or not we're aware of them and whether or not we've invited them into our life. These are the forces with a scope greater than is ours to claim, encompassing that which is beyond the control – and sometimes the understanding – of the individual. Here we have contact with the motivating forces in the universe. Here we confront the forces of time, fate, transformation, hope, balance, addiction, death, and immortality. Forces beyond the individual, indeed!

The often-misunderstood Personality, or Court Cards, depict attitudes, approaches, and various ways of being in and moving through the world. Each specific card points to a unique way of meeting personal needs, accomplishing goals, and expressing oneself. To have developed access to and facility with each of these sixteen personality traits is to have become a well-rounded individual with the ability to respond authentically to any and all situations.

These three sectors of dynamic energies are in constant interplay with one another, every day, all the time. This is a fact easily forgotten as we move through the mechanics of our daily routine. We're very often moving along on "auto pilot," comfortably maneuvering our established persona over well-worn pathways (that is to say, using a few select Personality Cards while engaging in only certain specific experiences among the 40 MINOR ARCANA), oblivious to the fact that archetypal and transformational energies are our constant companions.

The following method provides an opportunity to check in with the interplay between these three sectors of experience, allowing us to honor the different but related aspects of our being in any given situation.

The first matter of business with this method is to divide your deck into three piles: the 40 MINOR ARCANA cards, the 22 MAJOR ARCANA cards, and the 16 Personality Cards. Shuffle the cards in each pile, keeping the sector piles separate and distinct from one another. Then, decide which topic in your life you'd like to address by this method. Settle your mind, focus on your area of concern, and when you're ready, choose one card for each of the following positions:

Diagram #4

Card #1: chosen from the MINOR ARCANA pile. This describes an essential fact about the matter.

Card #2: chosen from the MAJOR ARCANA pile. This depicts the larger force at work in the matter.

Card #3: chosen from the Personality Card pile. This indicates the most effective approach to the matter.

Some thoughts to consider as you reflect on the meanings and the interactions between the cards appearing in this layout:

Where is there ease and/or harmony between any of the cards?

Where is there tension and/or stress between any of the cards?

Are there common themes, images, or symbols in the three cards?

What is the overall tone of the cards: Confident? Confused? Calm? Challenged? Transformational?

Do reversed cards appear? If so, what does the reversed position depict or imply?

Is there a confirmation of your thoughts/feelings/actions around the matter?

Regarding Card #1 MINOR ARCANA
Is this card familiar to you?
Does this card surprise you?
Does the card provide any new information about the matter?

Regarding Card #2 Major Arcana
Are you aware of this force as integral to the matter?
How much personal control over the matter does this force allow?
What is your relationship to this card, its significance and its indications?

Regarding Card #3 Personality Card
Is this attitude something with which you are familiar?
Does the card suggest a new approach?
Is it challenging for you to embrace the attitude of the card?
What does this card imply about your personal power within this matter?

Guidelines for
Expansion of the Layout

This is a relatively simple and self-contained layout. You may
want to draw one additional card for "What must I remember as
this matter unfolds?" but don't make this layout too complicated.
Take time to muse upon the three cards in the initial draw, pondering
the relationship between what is in your sphere of influence and what is
not, what can be managed and what needs to be allowed, where personal
will can be effective…and where patience may be required.

General Overview with World Card Spread

5-Card Layout

If you were to look at THE WORLD card in any traditional version of the Tarot, you would see representatives of the four elements of creation (as designated by the fixed signs of the zodiac: earth/Taurus bull, fire/Leo lion, air/Aquarian human, and water/Scorpio eagle) in each of the four corners, with an image of the integrated self at the center of the card. As card #21 in the MAJOR ARCANA series, THE WORLD card depicts the process of culmination and the harmonization of the disparate aspects of human nature.

The "World" layout is an overview method allowing an examination of the different elements intrinsic to a given situation. In particular, it provides an opportunity to look at the various ways by which different aspects of our personality are dealing with and managing the same issue.

We will use this basic pattern of four corners revolving around a central point, an image known to the alchemists as the "squaring of the circle," as a template for this layout. The squared circle is a quintessential image of wholeness and completion, making this layout well-suited for any matter where a balance and/or an integration of disparate elements is sought.

The designation of the positions within this layout is a bit more complex than what we've experienced thus far. In the previous methods, it's been relatively easy to determine the implications of "past-present-future" or "body-mind-spirit" and to interpret cards in terms of these easily-understood definitions.

With the "World" layout, a method which uses the four elements of creation as keys to the interpretation of each position, things are perhaps not quite as obvious. Not to worry: The four elements each have very specific, definitive, and unique energies.

Diagram #5

Card #3

Air

Card #4

Water

Card #5

Outcome
Goal
Purpose

Card #1

Earth

Card #2

Fire

Use these quick and easy ways to think about each of the positions within this layout:

Card #1: Earth (The Bull)
What is the state of practical matters in regard to the query?

Card #2: Fire (The Lion)
What is the state of my will, determination, and creativity in regard to the query?

Card #3: Air (The Human Mind)
What is the state of my thoughts, perceptions, and ideals in regard to the query?

Card #4: Water (The Eagle)
What is the state of my feelings and unconscious reality in regard to the query?

Card #5: Outcome
What is the outcome, goal, or purpose of the matter?

While all of this may seem like a lot of information to manage, it helps to remember that a card placed in a particular slot within the template offers a head start on interpretation. Take your time, be patient with yourself, and allow some space in your mind for intuition to speak. Once you are clear about the meanings of the positions within the spread, select the cards for the template.

Remember: Placing cards intentionally in their assigned positions is the name of the game.

Here are additional clarification points, thoughts to consider once you've placed cards into each of the positions and begin interpretation. Use these questions to help solidify your sense of each card's meaning as it appears within the layout:

Card #1: Earth
What is the general tone of this card?

What type of energy do I bring to the practical aspects of the matter?

Are the practical aspects of the matter in order?

Am I stable and centered regarding the matter?

How realistic am I being in regard to the matter?

How is my physical body reacting to the matter?

(How) are finances and other resources impacted by the matter?

Card #2: Fire
What is the general tone of this card?

What type of energy do I bring to the creative aspects of the matter?

How much energy is needed to resolve the matter?

Is originality and innovation being called upon?

Is there a struggle or conflict regarding the matter?

Is my will aligned with this matter or am I pulled in several different directions?

How hard will I have to fight for this resolution?

Card #3: Air
What is the general tone of this card?

What type of energy do I bring to the mental aspects of the matter?

What ideals or principles are operating in the matter?

What convictions do I hold regarding the matter?

How clear are my thoughts about the matter?

Do my world view and belief systems impact the matter?

What is the nature of communication with others about the matter?

Card #4: Water
What is the general tone of this card?

What type of energy do I bring to the emotional aspects of the matter?

What are my true feelings about this matter? What is intuition telling me?

(How) are emotions informing the situation?

Are relationships with other people coming into play?

How sincerely do I want to accomplish this goal?

Card #5: Goal/Purpose/Outcome
What is the general tone of this card?

What is the likely culmination of the matter?

What am I trying to accomplish?

Toward what resolution is the matter headed?

What is there to learn through this experience?

Aside from my wants and needs, what is trying to happen in regards to the matter?

In the "big picture," what do I need to know regarding this matter?

You'll gain information from each card in its individual position by using the above questions to help form a "field of meaning" for each card. But there is also information held in the connections between the cards and from the five cards as a group. It can be helpful to pay attention to these sorts of relationships between cards:

Are the elemental associations of the selected cards aligned with the nature of the positions? For instance, do you see a CUP card as Card #4 (Water), or a PENTACLE as Card #1 (Earth)?

What does it indicate if there is a difference between a card's elemental association and the nature of the position? For instance, if there is a SWORD card as Card #2 (Fire), what might that imply?

Is there a variety of elements within the layout, or do a few elements predominate the spread?

Do MAJOR ARCANA cards play a significant role in the reading?

Is there a particular card that stands out from the others, one that seems to carry more weight or importance?

Which card speaks the loudest to you, or draws your attention most strongly?

Does Card #5 (Goal/Purpose/Outcome) bring something new to consider?

Does Card #5 (Goal/Purpose/Outcome) seem like a reasonable or expected outcome given the existing situation?

Are the five cards as a group comfortable and/or familiar to you, or do they feel disparate or disharmonious?

Do reversed cards appear? If so, what does the reversed position depict or imply?

Do the cards as a group tell a particular story?

Does the reading provide advice?

Does the reading confirm what you already know?

Does the reading encourage you to bring new energies to any or all of the components of the situation?

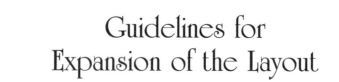

Guidelines for Expansion of the Layout

This can be a meaty layout offering up lots of information; guard against complicating it with too many side queries! Additional cards can always be drawn to clarify or elucidate any card already in the spread, and something akin to "What can help me be successful in this endeavor?" is always a fine way to wrap up a reading. But keep it simple. When it comes to the "World" layout, sticking close to the basic five-card template will make interpretation much more manageable.

General Overview & Goal-Setting Using the Star Spread

5-Card Layout

Since childhood, we've gazed and wondered at the stars, we have been awarded stars for our good work at school, and we've no doubt more than once wished upon a star. Astrologers for millennia have sought guidance about our most essential matters within the movements of the stars. THE STAR card in the Tarot is emblematic of our creative ability to manifest our most authentic selves here on planet earth. In these and its many other representations, the image of the star has become a primary symbol of our hopes, dreams, and highest aspirations. What a wonderful diagram to use as a framework for a Tarot layout!

In addition to being an effective template for any kind of general inquiry, this is an excellent layout with which to examine the factors involved in a future goal. As with the stars shown on most PENTACLE cards, we'll use a star diagram with the fifth point directed upward, keeping an eye toward honest, well-purposed actions and goals. (For further information regarding the STAR and the PENTACLE symbolism, see page 101) In this five-card layout, one card is placed on each of the segments of the star pattern, the purpose being to examine the factors involved in accomplishing a goal or attaining a specific outcome.

Diagram #6

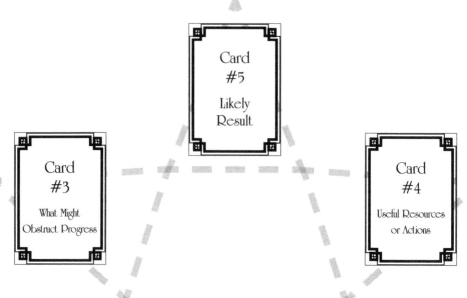

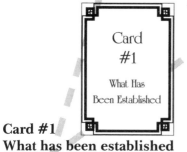

Card #1
What has been established

Card #2
What will need to be developed

Card #3
What might obstruct or hinder progress

Card #4
What are the most useful resources or best possible actions

Card #5
Likely result of this process

Use the following as intention guidelines for cards that are being selected for each position within the layout:

Card #1
What has already been established

> What tasks have been completed?

> What lessons have been learned?

> In what areas do I have competence?

> What have I built or created that supports me?

> What is the foundation for the next step?

Card #2
What will need to be developed

> What new abilities will be required?

> What new areas of learning may appear?

> What might I have to change?

> Where might there be risks?

> Where might I be stepping into the unknown?

Card #3
What might obstruct or hinder progress

> Who/what does not want to change?

> Are there outer forces that resist my efforts?

> Are there outworn habits that persist?

> Who/what might I have to overcome?

> Of what obstacles need I be aware?

Card #4
What are the most useful resources or best possible actions

Which of my abilities will best serve me?

What is my best course of action?

Who/what can help me?

In whom/what can I have confidence?

To whom/what must attention be directed?

Card #5
Likely result

What is the most likely evolution of the current situation?

What can be expected to occur?

For what should I be prepared?

What are the lessons to be learned from this experience?

What are the highest aspirations for the current situation?

Note that the "result" is not considered a written-in-stone inevitability, but rather the next natural step in an unfolding story.

As with the "World" layout (page 55), the assigned positions within the "Star" spread do much to inform us as to how to interpret the cards on the table. With the "Star" spread in particular, we have some useful interconnections between card positions that are important to regard:

What is the relationship between what has been established (Card #1) and what needs to be developed (Card #2)? Does something new need to be brought in? Will something need to be approached in a different manner?

Are you aware of the impact of your abilities upon the situation?

Are you challenged by what will need to be developed?

What is the relationship between what might hinder development (Card #3) and useful resources and best actions (Card #4)? Does something new need to be brought in? Will something need to be approached in a different manner?

What is your reaction/relationship to Card #3 (Hindrance or Obstruction)?

What is your reaction/relationship to Card #4 (Most Useful Resources)?

Is there a predominance of any one element within the spread?

Is there a prevalent theme to the reading? Do reversed cards appear? If so, what does the reversed position depict or imply?

Does the MAJOR ARCANA have a significant voice in the reading?

What does Card #5 (Likely Result) imply: A resolution? A "best approach?" Uncertainty? Options? Satisfaction?

Does the reading give any indication as to how to proceed?

Guidelines for Expansion of the Layout

This is a layout that is best kept intact without too much additional information being added, since the positions are relatively straightforward and work together efficiently within the diagram. But as always, you can draw a helper or clarifying card for any of the positions where further information is needed, by using questions such as "What can help me with this specific aspect?" or "What else do I need to know about this particular facet of the situation?"

Overview of a Specific Issue Using a Significator

5-Card Layout

A specific issue or concern can be examined in some depth by using an intentionally-chosen Significator card (a concept described on page 22) and a few well-chosen partners. By deliberately choosing a Significator which best suits the issue, you set the tone for the import of the reading, having thus provided a background within which to fill in the details of your picture.

Begin the choice of the Significator card by considering what it is you want to know. Be as clear and concise with yourself as you can be, since the reading will revolve around this initial concept. For instance, you may have a question about a relationship, but ...

Is your concern an emotional issue (a "Cups" issue) or a money issue ("Pentacle" issue) within the relationship?

Is it a question of love (Cups) or a question regarding the principles (Swords) of love?

If a particular person is involved, is there a Court Card that could be used as Significator?

Is your question about a specific relationship or relationships in general?

Is it a relationship in the present about which you're asking, or a relationship you hope to have in the future?

Do you have a question about your role in the relationship as a partner? As a parent? As a teacher? As an employer?

Once you've clarified your real issue, go through the entire deck –yes, all seventy-eight cards – looking at each card while keeping the query in mind. You will know instinctively which card is best for this query at hand...and don't be surprised if it's not the one you expected. Allow yourself to react intuitively to the card that wants to be chosen as Significator for any particular reading.

Using the intentionally selected Significator as the center of the wheel, draw the four additional cards at random from the 77 cards which remain in the deck, placing them in the following pattern:

Diagram #7

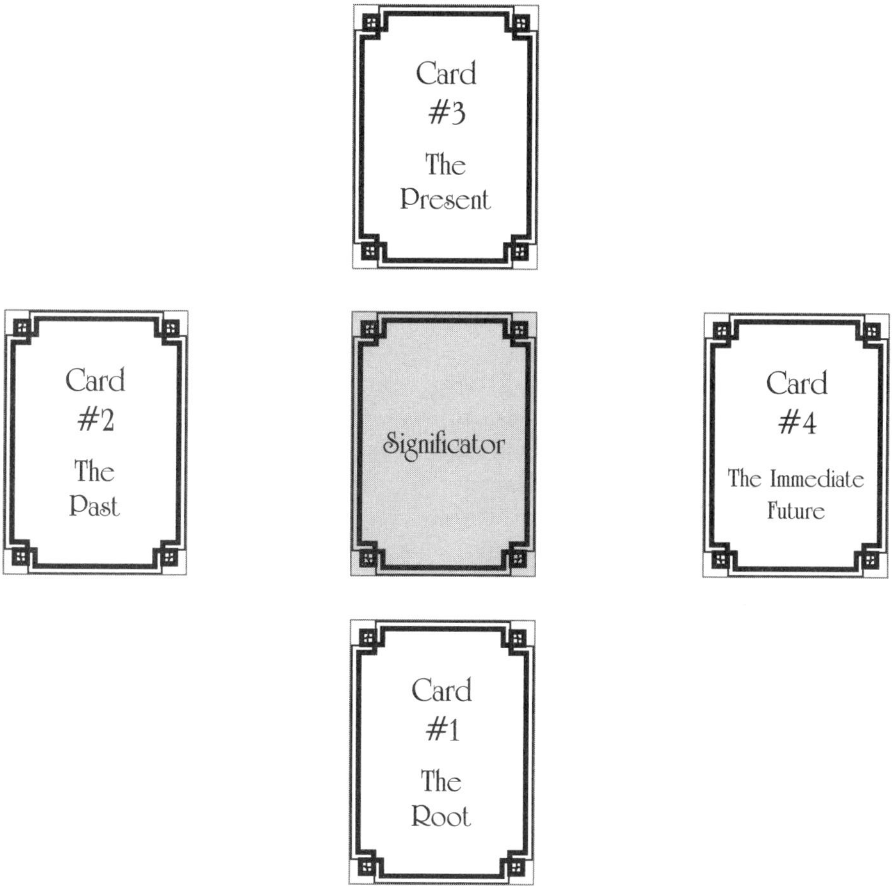

```
              ┌─────────────┐
              │   Card      │
              │   #3        │
              │   The       │
              │   Present   │
              └─────────────┘

┌─────────────┐ ┌─────────────┐ ┌─────────────┐
│   Card      │ │             │ │   Card      │
│   #2        │ │             │ │   #4        │
│   The       │ │ Significator│ │ The Immediate│
│   Past      │ │             │ │ Future      │
└─────────────┘ └─────────────┘ └─────────────┘

              ┌─────────────┐
              │   Card      │
              │   #1        │
              │   The       │
              │   Root      │
              └─────────────┘
```

Card #1: The Root

Card #2: The Past

Card #3: The Present

Card #4: The Immediate Future

All the cards chosen will revolve around and refer back to the Significator. The Significator is important in itself as the focal point of the reading, but becomes more "significant" as it develops relationships with the other cards that appear in the spread.

Let's further define the positions within this template so that we can more effectively understand the relationships between the cards that are drawn:

Card #1: The Root

This card represents what is at the core of the matter. Whatever is basic, essential, and intrinsic to the issue (as indicated by the Significator) will be shown in the card that appears here. You might look at Card #1 with these thoughts in mind:

Is this how/why the issue started?

Is this an unchangeable aspect of the issue?

Is this the lesson, challenge, opportunity, or goal of this issue?

Is this something that has been unseen and/or unacknowledged about the issue?

Is this an underlying theme to this issue?

Card #2: The Past

This card indicates a past experience regarding the matter, a specific event or experience having some bearing on the current state of affairs. Usually having occurred within the past six months and having relevance to the Significator in some fashion, Card #2 can be thought of in these terms:

What about that past experience is important to me now?

What did I learn from that experience?

Has the past event or experience been resolved?

How has this past experience shifted my perspective on the matter?

Was the past experience a stepping-stone of some sort in regard to the goals of the Significator?

Card #3: The Present

This card shows your current connection to the matter in question. What you are thinking, how you are feeling, what worries you, or where your confidence sits will show up in the card that appears here. Here are some pointers as you interpret Card #3:

How does the present situation look different from the past experience?

Has the experience of the past been resolved in/by the present situation?

Are my thoughts and feelings about the matter accurately depicted by this card?

What is the relationship between the present energy and the Significator?

Am I where I want to be in regard to the goals of the Significator?

Card #4: The Immediate Future

This card shows what might be the next evolution of the present energy. It indicates what is immediately ahead, and gives us a picture of what to expect in the very near future. When Card #3's energy shifts, it's apt to move toward something looking like what we see in Card #4. Things to think about with this position include:

What might be ahead as I try to accomplish the goals of the Significator?

Can I expect things to change in the next couple of weeks?

Do I see anything coming from an outside source that will shift the situation?

What is the best attitude as I move forward: Optimism? Caution? Bravery? Resignation? Empowerment?

Is there advice as to how to attain a successful resolution?

Once you've gotten a sense of the cards facing you, these thoughts might help you weave together the different components within the spread:

Is there a consistent theme among the cards or do you see many different pieces trying to work together?

What is the pace of the story that appears on the table: Swiftly moving? Stalled? Slow but steady?

Do you see an evolving story or is there "stopping and starting," u-turns, and/or lulls in the action?

Is there a preponderance of any one image, element, or of the MAJOR ARCANA?

Do the cards offer any suggestions or input regarding the outcome?

Is the theme of the Significator supported and reinforced by the surrounding cards?

Is the theme of the Significator diluted, strained, or pulled in another direction by the surrounding cards?

Do reversed cards appear? If so, what does the reversed position depict or imply?

Is there a new piece of the puzzle, something unexpected or as yet untested, which appears as part of the story?

Do the cards suggest that you advance proactively, or do they encourage a more receptive approach to the situation?

What is the general tone of what is trying to happen in terms of the Significator?

Guidelines for
Expansion of the Layout

The scope of this spread is fairly thorough, yet remains simplified given that the focus is on the meaning of the Significator and the forces directly impacting it. However, if you encounter gaps in meaning or want to develop other lines of query, here are some suggested lines of questioning:

If there are unresolved matters from the past, draw an additional card or two, placing them between Card #2 (The Past) and Card #3 (The Present), to provide further information or to help with closure.

Draw an additional card or two, placing them either above or below Card #3 (The Present), to help clarify questions about the present situation.

Draw a card or two, placing them between Card #3 (The Present) and Card #4 (The Immediate Future), as helpers or guides for moving forward in a positive manner.

Draw an additional card or two, placing them after Card #4 (The Immediate Future), for more information about what you might expect in the immediate future.

Draw an additional card to aid in the understanding of what is needed by the Significator in order to resolve the issue successfully.

Overview of a Specific Issue Using the Resolution Factor

3-Card Layout

"I'm stuck."

"I really don't know what to do."

"I can't seem to get anywhere."

"There doesn't seem to be a reasonable solution to this problem."

We've all experienced this place of tension and confusion, held captive by a situation with no sense of options and no hope for resolution. Maybe you've found yourself in a thankless work situation but have come to rely on the consistent income and health benefits. Perhaps a once-passionate relationship has devolved into dulling complacency. Or maybe life just isn't working out as planned, hoped, or expected. It's very easy to become so enmeshed with a problem that all perspective becomes lost. When this happens, "The Resolution Factor" layout can be a useful tool for clarification.

> **Important:** This layout is designed to resolve the tension around an issue, not necessarily to resolve the issue itself.

Not all problems have immediate and happy solutions; we'll need to keep that fact in mind as we work with this method. However, any problem can be ameliorated by a simple clue as to how to relieve the stress between "what is" and "what could be." This three-card layout allows an objective look at a problem so that a clear perspective can be restored.

Diagram #8

Card
#3

The
Resolution
Factor

Card
#1

You
in the Situation

Card
#2

The
Intrinsic Nature
of The Situation

Card #1
This card represents you in the situation.

Card #2
This card represents the intrinsic nature of the situation.

Card #3
This card represents the factor that can help resolve the tension be-
tween Card #1 and Card #2.

As you take an initial overview of the cards appearing within this layout, keep these concepts in mind:

Do common themes, suits, or symbols appear, and what might that imply?

What is the general tone of the reading as a whole: Disjointed? Combative? Uncomplicated? Obtuse? Direct? Other?

What does the reading suggest is the best course of action: Patience? Assertion? Collaboration? Other?

Where, if at all, do MAJOR ARCANA cards appear and what does this tell you?

If Personality cards are present, are they indicative of particular people, aspects of yourself, or both?

Do reversed cards appear? If so, what does the reversed position depict or imply?

Does any card show an aspect of which you are presently aware?

Does any card show something new that needs to be considered?

In particular, the following thoughts can help determine the message of each card as well as the relationships between the cards within the layout:

Is the depiction on Card #1 accurate for you?

Do you recognize the part you play in the depiction and/or message of Card #1?

If the implication of Card #1 is undesirable, is there anything you can do to change that?

Is Card #2 an accurate depiction of the situation?

Is new information brought to light through what is indicated by Card #2?

Are Card #1 and Card #2 similar in any way?

Is there an obvious opposition between Card #1 and Card #2?

Does Card #3 (the resolution factor) have a similarity to either Card #1 (you) or Card #2 (the situation)?

What does Card #3 (the resolution factor) bring to the situation that Card #1 (you) and Card #2 (the situation) have not provided?

Does Card #3 (the resolution factor) bring a new element or energy into the situation?

Does Card #3 (the resolution factor) imply a resolution to the issue as well as a resolution to the tension of the situation?

Guidelines for Expansion of the Layout

Because this is a bare-bones layout designed to reveal the key dynamics of an issue, expansion options should be kept to a minimum. Limit additional card draws to the following types of queries:

Draw one card in response to "What can help me implement the resolution factor?"

Draw one card in response to "What could be a potential block in the resolution of this situation?"

Draw one card in response to "What is my best resource in this situation?"

Draw one card in response to "What is my biggest challenge with this situation?"

Draw one card in response to "What do I need to remember as I move through this situation?

Relationship Spread
4-Card Layout

"Relationship" is the issue which brings the greatest number of visitors to the Tarot table. It's not just the love life that vexes us, but relationships with the in-laws, the kids, the boss, and the neighbors. If you actually began counting, you might be surprised at the number of people with whom you are in some sort of relationship.

Because they involve connections to other people, not to mention that fluid and slippery stuff we call "emotions," relationships are not only the most common topic at the Tarot table, they are the most complicated. Thankfully, there is an easy method with which to begin the untangling.

The beauty of the basic "Relationship" layout is that it does not begin with a question. (Relationships have enough questions as it is.)

Important: Begin this method by setting an intention to observe the dynamics between the people involved, and draw further lines of questioning from the information appearing there.

Some of your relationship questions will be addressed promptly by this initial procedure. At the same time, this is an excellent layout to be used in expanded forms for the garnering of additional information. The initial intention with this method is: "Show me the nature of the relationship between me and person X." Here is the basic pattern:

Diagram #9

 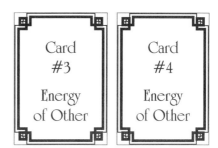

Card #1 and Card #2
These two cards represent you/your energy in the relationship

Card #3 and Card #4
These cards represent the other person/energy of the other person in the relationship

As a way of honoring and supporting yourself, it's a good idea to first draw the cards which will represent you, followed by the pair of cards for the other person. If you have questions about more than one person, use the above method for you and each participant as a separate layout.

> **Important:** Your connection to each person in your life is specific and unique. Don't assume that your energy is the same with Person X as it is with Person Y. Always draw two cards for yourself and two cards for the other person for each relationship in question.

What you'll see in the four cards on the table is a snapshot of the dynamics at work within the relationship: a description without judgment, without agenda, without emotional attachment. To be able to view the scenario in pictures, to look at it with objectivity…what a gift. Here are some things to think about during your interpretation:

What is it that each of us brings to the relationship?

Does the scenario that these four cards present confirm my thoughts and feelings?

Does the scenario that these four cards present surprise me in any way?

Is there balance and harmony within myself (as shown between Card #1 and Card #2) regarding the relationship?

Is there opposition or tension within myself (as shown between Card #1 and Card #2) regarding the relationship?

Is there balance and harmony in the other person (as shown between Card #3 and Card #4) regarding the relationship?

Is there opposition or tension within the other person (as shown between Card #3 and Card #4) regarding the relationship?

Are there similarities between the two sets of cards?

Are there disparities between the two sets of cards?

Is someone pushing? Is someone pulling? Is someone resisting? Is someone oblivious?

Is there any common bond between the two sets of cards?

Is there a propensity of a particular suit, or of the MAJOR ARCANA?

Do reversed cards appear? If so, what does the reversed position depict or imply?

Do the cards indicate people moving in different directions?

Do the cards reflect a conflict between heart and head? A battle of wills? A standoff? A waiting game?

Do the cards reflect partnership? Harmony? Sharing? Compassion? Love? Friendship?

If Personality (Court) Cards are present, are they facing each other? Facing away from one another? Reaching out? Ignoring one another? Communicating? Arguing? Connecting?

Isn't it amazing that such an impressive depth of information, confirmation, and clarification can arise from this simple layout?

Guidelines for Expansion of the Layout

Once the four primary cards are drawn, the relevant issues and ensuing questions will present themselves readily. "What is really going on in this relationship?" "Why is the other person holding back?" "How does the other person really feel about me?" "What can help this relationship flourish?" The Basic Relationship Layout lends itself very well to expansion and development, and it's perfectly fine to follow up on whatever lines of questioning the first group of cards presents, being clear and intentional (as always) about your questions. Some thoughts for expansion of the initial template include:

Draw a single card in response to "What do I need to know and remember about this relationship?"

Draw a card or two in response to "What does this relationship bring to my life?"

Draw a single card in response to "What is my best approach to this relationship?"

Draw a single card in response to "What might help this relationship flourish?"

Draw a single card in response to "What might be hindering this relationship from further development?"

For inquiries with a bit more complexity:

Draw one or two cards in response to "What does the other person need from me?"

Draw one or two cards in response to "How can I support myself in this relationship?"

Draw a card or two in response to "What can I do to make the most of this relationship?"

Draw a card or two in response to "What is the purpose of (or lesson with) my relationship with this person?"

Draw a card or two in response to "What issue(s) is/ are being worked out in this relationship?"

Draw two cards in response to "What can I expect from this relationship in the immediate future?"

The "Relationship" layout is a particular method in which we need to remember one of the Tarot No-No's mentioned in an earlier chapter: Keep clear boundaries and mind your manners. Use of the Tarot as a tool for conscious living allows us to inquire about people and matters having direct connection to and impact upon us. Peering into situations that exist between other people is rude and unacceptable.

Questions of Time and Timing
4- to 8-Card Layout

"When will my house sell?"
"When will I be able to retire?"
"How long will Joan and I be married before we have a baby?"
"When will my soul mate come into my life?"
Queries regarding time and timing can be so intricate, and for so many reasons!

First of all, most queries beginning with the word "when" need to be rephrased. "When" is a four-letter word when it comes to Tarot queries! If this is the first word in any question posed to the cards, take a moment to recognize whether responsibility has been accepted for the state of the matter, or if it has already been handed over (prematurely?) to the forces of destiny. For instance, before asking "When will my house sell?" you could have asked yourself:

Have I done all I can to make the house attractive, safe, and ready for sale?

Am I absolutely sure that I'm ready and willing to sell the house?

Am I happy with the realtor, or whoever is selling the house?

Do I have somewhere to live once the house sells?

Does it make financial good sense to be selling the house?

> **Important:** It isn't effective to delve into the "when" of a situation before doing some research into the back story, before looking into the various factors that have an impact on the issue.

Looking at another example, let's say the query is about Joan having a baby. One might take into consideration questions such as these before looking at "when" a pregnancy might occur:

Are Joan and I in agreement about wanting to have children?

Are Joan and I in agreement about how we plan to raise children?

Are there any known physical reasons that Joan and I might be unable to have children?

Are there work or financial issues that might impact our decision to have a child?

What do we need to know in order to be ready for parenthood?

This type of preliminary groundwork determines the readiness of an issue to be placed into the hands of timing and fate; be wary of any "when" question that hasn't first covered these bases.

Beyond this, after you've acknowledged and tended to the background information behind any "when" question, it's likely that the query will yet need rephrasing. Keeping the matter of one's personal power in mind, notice how the question "When will I be able to retire?" is different from "What needs to happen (or what can I do) so that I will be able to retire?" Or, how is the implication of "When will my soul mate come into my life?" different from that of "What can I do to support, allow, and encourage my soul mate to come into my life?" One question calls forth the random hand of fate, the other offers assistance in the effort to create a desired outcome.

> **Important:** Always phrase a query in such a way that empowerment of the individual, self-directed autonomy, and personal will are engaged toward the most positive outcome.

Of course we can't always get what we want. Neither does asking a question nicely (or appropriately) ensure the desired outcome. But the importance of conferring personal power within a query cannot be underestimated. To do so draws the line between using the Tarot as a fortune-telling tool (a craft at which very few folks are truly gifted) and the development of a consciously and intentionally created life, a capability which we all possess.

Alright. You've done your homework regarding the factors affecting the outcome of your query. Now we will address how to explore matters of time and timing within a Tarot reading.

A significant problem with queries regarding time and timing is that the concept of "time" is a relative term. Modern science, quantum physics, and Albert Einstein all confirm to us that time is flexible and fluid, not to mention subjective and relative. Those people who do channeling work with spirit guides, or those who access "higher" realms of consciousness, consistently communicate the idea that, in the "other world" there is no such thing as time or space.

The notion that time is immaterial is a mind-bender for sure, for us humans who are attached to the wrist watch, the clock, the calendar, the season, the number of years we've lived, and the time we have available in which to accomplish our goals. With the various factors of consciousness, science, and the cosmic nature of reality in play, it's no wonder that a determination of timing within a reading is tough to pin down and predict accurately.

The "when" question stands smack dab in the path of many a desired result. So, rather than fight this beastly matter head on, we'll do what any ingenious traveler would do – take another route and approach the result from a different angle. Instead of asking "when will this happen?" and drawing cards in search of an answer, we'll begin by drawing cards intentionally for the "when" and then look for our answer within those parameters.

Important: The first step this method regarding time and timing is to assess which time frame best suits the question.

You'll need to consider if the desired outcome can be expected within a matter of days, weeks, months, seasons, or years. Determining the appropriate parameter helps to set the intention as you begin to unravel the puzzle of "when."

For instance, if you were working with the question "When will my soul mate come into my life?" you might decide to look at four increments of time which encompass the next four seasons. (That is, of course, after you decided if you really wanted a soul mate and if you believed in such a thing in the first place.) If such a query was posited during the winter, the question would then be phrased such as "Do I see this event occurring this spring? Do I see this event occurring this summer? Do I see this event occurring this autumn? Do I see this event occurring next winter?" *Note: When using a time increment of the seasons, use the calendar definition of the season to avoid any miscommunication. For instance, many people would say that summer is over after Labor Day, when in fact summer technically ends on September 22ⁿᵈ.*

As a sample query for this layout, let's use the question, "It is now April and my house is on the market. I'm wondering when I might expect it to sell."

With this query, we might consider it reasonable that the house would sell within the next four months. With that clarification (and intention) in mind, we draw two cards for each of the next four months and look for indications within those four monthly increments of a house sale.

Once you've chosen time frames to use as parameters for the particular issue (days/weeks/months/ etc...), draw two cards each for up to four consecutive increments of the selected time frame. In the example regarding the sale of the house, then, the layout would look like this:

Diagram #10

Card #1 and Card #2
These show the likelihood of the house selling in May

Card #3 and Card #4
These show the likelihood of the house selling in June

Card #5 and Card #6
These show the likelihood of the house selling in July

Card #7 and Card #8
These show the likelihood of the house selling in August

Especially with matters of timing, you want to keep the query framed in terms of likelihoods and probabilities, rather than absolute terms. What can I expect? For what should I be prepared? What is the tenor of this process? These are the appropriate mind-sets when approaching any inquiry dealing with time.

Some helpful ideas as you process the cards that appear within the chosen parameters include:

Do I see an outcome of any sort within the parameters drawn?

Do the cards show any indication of additional required actions on my part?

Is there encouragement for the desired outcome?

Are there suggestions for realigning myself with a new outcome?

Are there suggestions for improving the outcome?

Must I be patient or does the reading suggest a quick resolution?

What does this potential outlook encourage me to do/plan/think?

Guidelines for Expansion of the Layout

Because the initial definitions of the positions are specific and direct, this layout is best kept simplified and expansion should be kept to a minimum. Limit additional cards to those drawn as "helper cards" for any areas where the card's message is confusing, or as guides and support for the solidification of any aspect that seems likely to work out positively.

Two Additional Methods for Matters of Timing

There are two additional easy methods for ascertaining matters of time and timing, both of which are useful and effective as long as they suit your style of reading. In addition, as exceptions to the general rule and because they utilize a very specific indicators of time, the use of the word "when" will be allowed!

Method One

The first alternative is a literal approach to the visual images on the cards, a method in which you allow the pictorial clues on the card to lead toward an interpretation. Let's use the above-mentioned query about a house sale, and draw a single card to answer the question "when will the house sell?"

Does the card show a winter scene, one of summer, or something less specific? Does the landscape shown on the card look like any particular month or time of year? Does the number on the card provide any hints as to "when?" For instance, if the EIGHT OF WANDS is drawn, could that indicate resolution within eight days or eight weeks or eight months?

Does the activity within the card suggest any particular time frame? For instance, are people on the card planting, harvesting, rejoicing, sleeping?

What other visual clues appear and what do they convey: Is the wind blowing through the card? Is the sun shining? Is it night time? Stormy weather? Do reversed cards appear? If so, what does the reversed position depict or imply?

What other information does the picture on the card convey, either literally or intuitively, regarding the issue of "when?"

It is true that cards can be very literal in the communication of their message, and so it's always a good idea to keep a lookout for the actual depiction of certain events as they occur on the face of the cards.

Method Two

A second additional method for determining the timing of a particular outcome or event involves acquainting yourself with the astrological associations for each card. This is not a practical or appealing method for everyone, but for those readers with knowledge of or an interest in astrology, this connection can provide a wide variety of informational streams.

The connection between Tarot and astrology is such that each of the seventy-eight cards of the Tarot has an association with an astrological sign and/or planet; additionally, the astrological signs and planets have correlations to specific parts of the calendar year. Therefore, the knowledge of the astrological designations for each Tarot cards allows for some very specific interpretations around issues of time and timing.

For instance, the Two of Swords relates to the first decan of Libra, or the dates between September 23rd and October 2nd. The Queen of Pentacles is associated with the sign of Taurus, the time period between April 21st and May 20th. The Moon card is ruled by Pisces, the days between February 19th and March 20th. These are very specific time increments indeed! (Mary K. Greer's quintessential Tarot manual, *Tarot for Your Self* [see List of Resources] is a wonderful resource for this type of information.)

> **Caution:** Take care not to extend any inquiry too far forward in time.

Things have a habit of changing; the more time involved, the more variables there are at play. Don't let your present to be much-influenced by a fluid and uncertain future.

Secondly, remember that things rarely are written in stone, even when we use the best tools possible and are respectfully mindful of the vagaries of time. It's the nature of the beast that matters regarding time are sticky wickets, being that the very notion of "time" is flexible, relative and changeable. We must take any time and timing reading with a notion of possibility lightly tinged with expectation. Many a querent has left the office of a reader having been told that love was coming in October, only to find out it wasn't this October but the one seven years hence.

Choices & Decision-Making

4- to 8-Card Layout

We live in an "either-or" culture, one which thrives on logic and rational decision-making. There isn't much else that is acknowledged, let alone valued, as being important to the decision-making process. This black-and-white way of thinking is at the root of much dysfunction and unhappiness, and the Tarot should not be used to reinforce this misguided and limited world view. Not in this or any other layout are we going to use the Tarot to tell us what is a "good" choice or a "bad" one. How, then, can we evaluate options so as to make positive choices?

There are ways of looking at options by means of the Tarot, manageable methods by which to view any situation with an objective and open mind so that informed decisions can be made. With the reminder that we always have at least a modicum of creative control in our lives, let's examine a simple layout by which to clarify choices and evaluate options.

When there is a choice to be made, there are options from which to choose: "Would it be wise to move to Atlanta or better to stay in Boston?" "Is it in my best interest to go to medical school at this time or keep my job and continue working?" "Between Alex, Steve, and Mary, who would make a good partner for me in my new business venture?"

Important: The keys to the "Choices" layout are in the definitions of the arenas in which you have choice and in the viability of the available options.

Begin this layout by defining the options as you've considered them thus far, articulating as many variables as there may be.

Sample query: Let's say you're considering a move to another city, and have narrowed the search down to Atlanta, San Francisco, Chicago, and Boston. Using an open-ended question such as "What is the likely quality of life if I were living in City X?" Draw two cards for each of the four designated cities. The question is not "Is it good for me to move to Atlanta?" or "Should I move to Boston?" Rather, it is an impartial look at what each city may have in store should a move to that locale take place.

> **Important:** Look at all options with equal objectivity in the initial phase of the reading.

In this example then, the layout would look like this:

Diagram #11

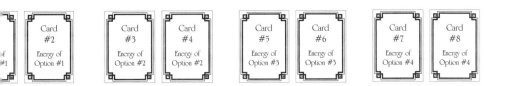

Cards #1 and #2
These represent the likely outcome of Option #1 (Atlanta)

Cards #3 and #4
These represent the likely outcome of Option #2 (San Francisco)

Cards #5 and #6
These represent the likely outcome of Option #3 (Chicago)

Cards #7 and #8
These represent the likely outcome of Option #4 (Boston)

The method here, regardless of the matter in question, is to draw two or three cards for each of the options within your query, and then to look with objectivity at the overall tone of that choice:

What is the general energy around each option?

What is the feeling sense of each option?

Do you like the looks of what is possible in any or all of the options?

What is your intuitive reaction to the options as they appear?

What additional questions arise about the options shown?

As stated in an earlier chapter, don't confuse this or any other method with too many "ifs." Keep the various options clear in your mind and try to limit them to four per reading. Too many cards muddy the message and may lead to a more confused state of mind – the opposite of what we're trying to achieve!

Once you've drawn cards for all the options within the initial query, use these guidelines as you interpret the options as they appear on the table:

Is there any one option that is clearly more desirable than the others?

Is there any one option that is clearly less desirable than the others?

Are there similarities between any of the options?

Are there significant discrepancies between the options?

Does the reading confirm what you had thought and felt about each option?

Does the reading bring any surprising or unexpected aspects to light?

Do any of the options have a mixed message, showing both "pro" and "con" to consider?

Where do the elements appear within the options and what does that tell you?

Do reversed cards appear? If so, what does the reversed position depict or imply?

Are financial or security issues brought to light?

Are relationship or family issues brought to light?

Do MAJOR ARCANA cards appear and what do they tell you?

You will discover that the Tarot is likely to support the notion that there is not a clear-cut "good choice" vs. "bad choice" scenario from which to choose. There is often a bit of each that is intrinsic to any matter. Much to our surprise and possible chagrin, the cards sometimes depict instances when it really doesn't matter one bit what we decide. Eventually you will confront a reading indicating that any choice will work out fine...or that any choice will likely have its challenges.

That there is not always a "do this and don't do that" circumstance is a fact that our rational mind might have trouble accepting. "But there must be a RIGHT choice!" we may secretly avow. This thought brings us back to the idea of the "either-or" cultural construct, as well as the importance of our world view and how it informs not only our questions but how we interpret our answers. Do you believe that there is a more "right" answer than the one that feels correct to you? Is there another answer beyond what your own knowing tells you? Your response to those posits will inform your interpretation of what is seen in this (and any other) layout.

Guidelines for Expansion of the Layout

This basic method for working with matters of choice allows some room for expansion, but if you're already looking at a number of options, it's best to keep this reading simple and to the point. Consider these types of queries when you need additional advice in decision-making:

Draw one or two cards in response to "What do I need to know about this decision?"

Draw one or two cards in response to "What do I need to remember as I make this decision?"

Draw one or two cards in response to "What might hinder a successful decision in this matter?"

Draw one or two cards in response to "What can help me make the best decision for myself?"

Draw one or two cards in response to "What are my best resources in this situation?"

Draw one or two cards in response to "What might be the purpose or goal of this decision for me?"

Draw one card in response to "What guiding principle can help me make a decision with the most positive result?"

Physical Health & Wellbeing Using the Chakra Spread
7-Card Layout

As we get older, we understand what our grandparents meant when they said, "If you have your health, you have everything." It turns out they were right, since without the physical body to support us, we truly are nowhere: personal will is ineffective, desires are left unmanifested, consciousness is left without a container.

Matters of health and well-being can be addressed by the Tarot, but this is an area where we have to be especially mindful to use all possible common sense combined with intellectual and intuitive knowing. The Tarot can alert us to potential problem areas within the body as well as point the way toward health and wellness, but should never be used as the last word regarding any issue, be it physical, mental, or otherwise.

> **Important:** Use the Tarot to turn your attention to potentially problematic physical issues, as well as toward avenues of healthy well-being. Do not use the Tarot to confer the final diagnosis on any matter.

Having said that, think what a marvelous tool the Tarot can be for the detection or confirmation (and the motivation for appropriate medical follow up) of weak spots in our physical body, places where we may either physically or intuitively feel that things are "not quite right" or "a little off" or "out of sorts." The seven-card "Chakra" spread is a basic layout which can be used to tune-in to energy as it exists in various parts areas of the body.

The chakra system itself, the diagram of which is the template for this layout, is an Eastern conceptualization of the major energy centers within the body. Each of these centers has a specific and unique function within the body, and each has a particular color of the spectrum associated with it. The "Chakra" spread diagram and a description of the positions within the spread are defined as follows:

Diagram #12

Card #1
The First, or Root Chakra (Red)
The root chakra is associated with the notion of personal security and safety, of groundedness and stability, comfort with one's physicality, and overall well-being. Bodily associations here are with the feet, legs, and seat.

Card #2
The Second, or Sacral Chakra (Orange)
The second chakra is where the "urge to merge" resides, deep attractions, what you take in and assimilate, sexual energy as well as nurturance. Bodily associations include the intestines, "what is in your gut," and the womb.

Card #3
The Third, or Solar Plexus Chakra (Yellow)
The third chakra is the seat of power, the place from which personal will emerges, as well as vitality, creativity, and ego strength. Bodily associations here are the stomach and digestive tract.

Card #4
The Fourth, or Heart Chakra (Green)
The fourth chakra is the mediating energy center (three chakras are above it, three are below.) This is the home of compassion and empathy, loving emotions and understanding. Bodily associations are with the heart and lungs.

Card #5
The Fifth, or Throat Chakra (Blue)
The fifth chakra is the place of voice, self-expression, and communication. What is said – as well as what is not said – resides here. Bodily associations are the neck, throat, and mouth.

Card #6
The Sixth, or "Third Eye" Chakra (Indigo)
The sixth chakra is the seat of sight: perceptions, visions both literal and figurative, knowing, and intuition. Bodily associations are the eyes, forehead, and brain.

Card #7
The Seventh, or Crown Chakra (Violet)
The seventh chakra allows access to transpersonal levels of knowing, of healing, and a connection to the ultimate Source of power and life. The seventh chakra resides at the very top of the head.

The "Chakra" layout is one before which it is particularly wise to take a few moments to relax and center oneself. Tuning in to the body through the Tarot is much more effective when a person is rested, calm, and mentally quiet before drawing cards.

This also is a spread where the manner by which the cards enter the layout is subject to personal preference. You may want to deal the cards from the top of deck, starting at Card #1 (The Root) and moving consecutively along through to Card #7 (The Crown). Or, you may choose to draw the cards individually from a random pile, first focusing your mind on a certain chakra and then "going fishing" for the card that speaks to you intuitively for that position. In a reading where the fact that the Tarot mirrors our reality is a very physical and material matter, it is important that the cards are selected with confidence and ease.

Once the cards are in defined positions within the spread, take a look at the grouping as a whole and consider these thoughts:

What is the primary tone or sense of the seven cards as a group?

Which major themes or recurring images or concepts present themselves?

What cards predominate the layout?

Do any cards line up particularly well with the significance of the position, i.e., is there an earthy card as Card #1 (The Root), or a fiery card as Card #3 (The Solar Plexus)?

Are there correlations between the cards in their positions and the associated colors for that position?

Where do you see harmony between any one card(s) and the one(s) adjacent?

Where do you schism or differentials between any one card(s) and the one(s) adjacent?

Where, if at all, do cards of strength and power appear?

Where, if at all, do cards of weakness or insecurity appear?

Where, if at all, do you see an easy relationship between adjacent cards?

Where, if at all, do you see energy blocks or breaks?

Where, if at all, does MAJOR ARCANA energy appear?

Is there a propensity of any one element?

Is any one element conspicuously absent?

Where do Personality Cards appear and to whom/what does that refer?

Do reversed cards appear? If so, what does the reversed position depict or imply?

Are there places in the diagram that correspond to any physical discomfort you may be experiencing?

Once the overall impact of the spread has been viewed and considered, the particular aspects of each card within its place in the diagram can be responded to and interpreted. Here are some guidelines for use as cards in their respective positions are reviewed:

Card #1: The Root
What does the card appearing here indicate regarding these types of issues:

What level of personal security do I experience?

How comfortable am I in my physical body?

Is there confidence in the ability to provide for myself?

Do I trust that the world will support my efforts?

How effectively am I relating to others around me?

Am I able to be solidly present in the given moment?

Do I connect to the notion that my physical presence makes a difference in the world?

Card #2: The Sacrum
What does the card appearing here indicate regarding these types of issues:

How am I assimilating my experiences at the moment?

To whom or what am I deeply connected?

Who/what is attracting my core energy?

Is what I am taking in/taking on helpful to me?

Is what I am taking in/taking on hindering or blocking me?

To what degree am I integrating my experiences?

Is there a yearning to nurture someone or something?

Card #3: The Solar Plexus

What does the card appearing here indicate regarding these types of issues:

What is the level of my focus and drive?

How am I managing my creativity?

What is the state of my ego strength?

Am I experiencing a self-directed life?

Is my personal will being used effectively?

Is self-expression finding an outlet?

Is anger or frustration spilling out of me?

Card #4: The Heart

What does the card appearing here indicate regarding these types of issues:

To what degree is my heart open to others?

Which matters touch my heart?
What is the current level of compassion for myself?

What is the current level of compassion for others?

Is there hope and optimism in my heart?

What inspires and encourages me?

To what degree do I empathize and support others?

Card #5: The Throat
What does the card appearing here indicate regarding these types of issues:

Am I communicating effectively?

Am I speaking my truth?

Do I "bite my tongue?"

Do I say what I mean?

Do I mean what I say?

What values are expressed in my words?

Do I take opportunities to speak freely?

Card #6: Third Eye
What does the card appearing here indicate regarding these types of issues:

How do I perceive the world?

What belief systems inform my reality?

Is my dream life activated?

Do I possess a sense of wonder and possibility?

Am I aware of the power of intuition?

What is the state of my conscious mind?

To what degree are thoughts and ideas impacting my life?

Card #7: The Crown
What does the card appearing here indicate regarding these types of issues:

What role is spirituality currently playing in my life?

To what degree am I spiritually connected?

Am I accessing information and knowledge from a source outside myself?

Am I open to "higher" levels of awareness?

Am I willing to look beyond myself and what is familiar for guidance?

Do I believe in the existence of a higher power?

How do I recognize the voice of a higher power?

Guidelines for Expansion of the Layout

There is a lot of information to keep track of with this spread, so try to keep any additional questions to a minimum. The draw for guiding cards around specific issues is a good approach, using basic methods such as:

Draw one or two cards as helpers or guides for any area within the layout that seems problematic, using questions such as "What is at the root of this issue?" or "What can help me best resolve this issue?"

Draw one or two cards as helpers or guides for any area within the layout that you'd like to enhance or encourage, using questions such as "What can help me build on this energy?" or "What do I need to remember in order to maintain positive energy in this area?"

Draw one card as an overview or helper card for guidance toward general well-being.

Work Issues &
Money Matters Using
the Pentacle Spread
5-Card Layout

When thinking about work issues in general and money issues in particular, we need to remember that, at their core, money issues are rarely about money. One's relationship with money is inextricably tied to emotions about money, expectations about money, cultural mores regarding money, one's family history with money, and the misconceptions about how much money one can have, deserves, or is capable of generating. We'll need to keep these intricacies in mind as we look at queries involving work, finances, and material security.

In Tarot, the tangible aspects of life are the realm of the suit of PENTACLES. In the old European Tarot decks, what we now call "PENTACLES" was referred to as "COINS," a nomenclature with a connotation to currency which limits our perception of the suit to this day. We often misunderstand (and underestimate) the suit of PENTACLES because, just like money issues, the suit of PENTACLES is not just about coins.

The PENTACLE itself tells us what we need to know about what the symbol means: a five-pointed star with the fifth point aimed skyward. In Tarot terms, four of the PENTACLE's points represent the four elements of creation: fire, air, water, and earth. The fifth point (the skyward point) signifies the "fifth essence," the "quint-essential" presence of Spirit, the force which gives life to, thereby animating and motivating, the four building-blocks (the four elements) of creation.

And so, ironically, it turns out that the Tarot suit with direct ties to our most tangible concerns is also the suit which most directly connects us to our spiritual nature! This is the essential implication of the PENTACLE cards within the Tarot: the recognition that material life is infused with, linked to, and a reflection of a spiritual reality.

PENTACLES, then, *are* about money, but are also about so many other parts of life. The realm of PENTACLES encompasses anything and everything which impacts material security, financial or otherwise: physical health, a sense of community and relatedness to others, the grounded and stable force that is projected as one moves through the world, and the degree to which one is able to manifest individual values and intentions. Whatever is created in the material world (that is to say, the result of the manner in which PENTACLES have been directed) is a direct reflection of self-worth, connection with others, and trust in the larger forces in the universe to support the effort. That's money and a whole lot more!

In homage to its lineage regarding coins, and because of its quintessential nature, we will use the line diagram of the PENTACLE as the outline for our work-related spread. (Reminding us once again that how we manifest the four building blocks of life, i.e., the four elements, will ultimately reflect spiritual values.) But first, one more point needs to be made regarding questions of work and finances, and it has to do with the dual nature of both PENTACLES and money issues.

Important: It is of vital importance when asking questions about money, finances, security, or any other practical matter, that one deliberates upon and determines the *real* question.

Any time we are looking at a change in job, career, or finances, a clarification of the essential goal or reason for making that change needs to be made. Think of the myriad ways to approach a work-related question:

What can I do to increase income?

How can I bring greater creativity into my work life?

Would a job or career change allow a move to a different city or part of the country?

How can I obtain a job with a better social standing?

How can I find work that is intellectually stimulating?

How do I find a job that makes me happy?

How can I be happier in the job I currently have?

What steps need to be taken in order to retire in five years?

How can I obtain enhanced benefits from my job, such as more vacation time or a better insurance package?

What can I do to augment the security and stability of the job I now have?

Is it in my best interest to look for different work?

What are the personal skills and abilities that can help me be successful?

What might be the qualities of the "ideal job" for me?

Would self-employment be a viable option for me?

How can I discover work that will feed my soul?

No "right" or "wrong" questions here, but many different questions with different agendas, motivations, and outcomes. It's likely that several of these parameters come into play given any possible change about which one might be musing. It's important to prioritize wants and needs, and consider these types of questions before applying the query to the layout. As we know, without a clear question it's very difficult to obtain a clear answer.

Once you've clarified the motivating factors and have posited a query, the PENTACLE diagram will serve as the vehicle for the reading. The first four positions indicate how personal resources and energies are being utilized in the specific situation; the fifth position reflects a goal, purpose, or "higher" message for the situation. Use the following to help guide your intention in selecting cards for this layout:

Diagram #13

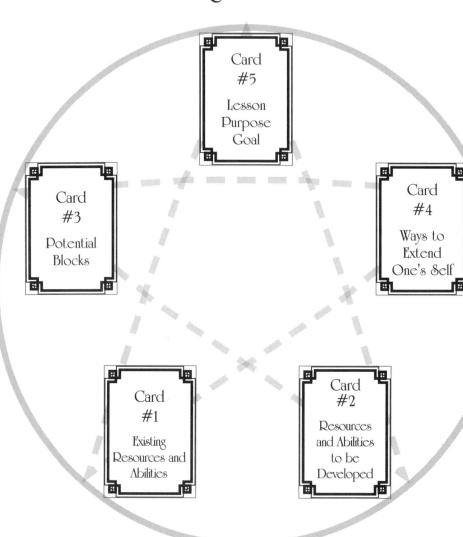

Card #1
What resources and/or abilities do I bring to the situation?

Card #2
What resources and/or abilities will need to be developed or expanded?

Card #3
What might be blocking the attainment of this goal?

Card #4
How might I be required to extend myself in order to attain this goal?

Card #5
What is the lesson or highest purpose of this goal or this situation?

As with many other spreads and layouts, it's a good idea to take a birds-eye view to gather the overall tone of the reading before getting into the particulars of interpretation. The definitions of the positions are self-explanatory, but general themes such as the following can be considered as you interpret the five cards within the layout:

Does any one element predominate the scene?

Do MAJOR ARCANA cards appear, and what do they indicate?

Do Personality cards appear and to whom/what do they refer?

Do reversed cards appear? If so, what does the reversed position depict or imply?

In particular, do PENTACLES appear in this query?

In addition to PENTACLES, what elements are at play and what does that indicate about the issue?

Where within the layout are the points of power and confidence?

Where within the layout are the places of insecurity and doubt?

Where are there compatibilities between cards?

Where are there disparities between cards?

Which talents or abilities does the reading confirm?

Does the reading provide support and optimism for the desired outcome?

Does the reading encourage patience and endurance?

Does the reading suggest the need for a change of plan?

Does the reading speak to the practical and rational aspects of the situation?

Does the reading speak to "higher" goals and aspirations?

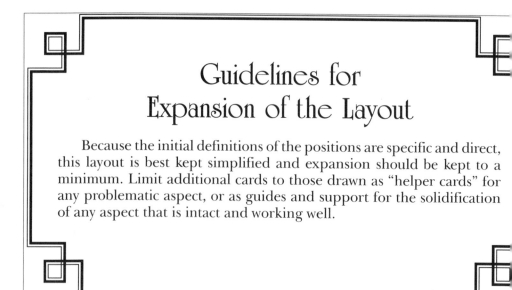

Guidelines for Expansion of the Layout

Because the initial definitions of the positions are specific and direct, this layout is best kept simplified and expansion should be kept to a minimum. Limit additional cards to those drawn as "helper cards" for any problematic aspect, or as guides and support for the solidification of any aspect that is intact and working well.

Completion / Closure Spread
5-Card Layout

Endings. Sometimes we're ready for them and sometimes they catch us by surprise. We may be relieved when they arrive; it may take years to recover from their presence.

Although many endings are brutally sad, not all endings are intrinsically painful. Sometimes endings, such as graduations and retirements, are satisfying. Sometimes, as in the ending of one's single life on one's wedding day, they are joyful. Sometimes there is a maze of emotions, such as one might experience upon moving to a new part of the country once grown children have left the nest. The following layout allows expression of the various aspects of any ending, and provides a context within which the experience can be acknowledged, honored, and released.

The template for this spread will be a square with a point at the center. As a form with four sides and four corners, the square is an image of solidity, structure, and power. Relevant to our purposes here, it's important to note that the number "4" has been cemented in the Western psyche as a conceptualization of "entirety" – the four directions of the compass, the four seasons, the four sections of an orchestra, the four chambers of the heart, the four quarters in a dollar, the four apostles, the four blood groups, and of course the most Fab of Fours, the Beatles.

Observable reality and pop culture aside, the number "4" is a significant force within the Tarot system, having not one, but three MAJOR ARCANA cards to express its different aspects. The first and most obvious aspect is THE EMPEROR, card number "4." Here sits the archetype of the builder, the patriarch, the creator of form and order. THE EMPEROR is the ruler of the four corners of the world, master of the four elements, builder of society's foundations, founder of business and organizations.

The second "4" in the Tarot is the DEATH card. Assigned number "13" in the MAJOR ARCANA series (keep in mind that 1+3=4), the DEATH card represents the force that breaks down whatever THE EMPEROR has built. Foundations, structures, laws, mores, physical bodies, it matters not to the DEATH card. All the world's forms eventually and inevitably yield to the undeniable force of card number "13."

The void created by the dismantling of the "4" by the "13" creates a space for new life. The impetus for what can fill this void comes with THE FOOL, MAJOR ARCANA card Zero. But THE FOOL is also card number "22, thus coming back around to "4" by the fact that 2+2=4. THE FOOL arrives after the culmination of THE WORLD card (MAJOR ARCANA #21) and before the creative spark of THE MAGICIAN (MAJOR ARCANA #1) in a unique "alpha and omega" placement. THE FOOL is both the ultimate goal and the motivational force for the goal in the first place; paradoxical, irrational, and esoteric as its coinciding number Zero.

These three archetypes, then, THE FOOL/EMPEROR/DEATH, express the form of the material world in its various states of manifestation. Each with a numerological connection to the number "4," as a group they depict the regenerative cycle that exists between the life spark, the act of creation, and the process of decay, a cycle that is the essence of our physical reality.

This is a lengthy explanation as to why the form of a square is being used as the foundation for the "Closure" spread. If we're intending to deal with matters of closure, we must look at the form, structure, and context (the "4") whose passing we acknowledge.

To use the form of a square as the template for the "Closure" spread pays respect to the dynamic forces within the life cycle, but although we start with the four sides of the square, the archetype of change and closure transmutes a four-sided form into an image with five components.

Here are the assignments of meaning for each of the positions within the spread:

Card #1
What did I bring to the experience?

Card #2
What did I learn from the experience?

Card #3
What can I now leave in the past?

Card #4
What do I bring forward from the experience?

Card #5
What was the lesson/purpose of the experience?

Diagram #14

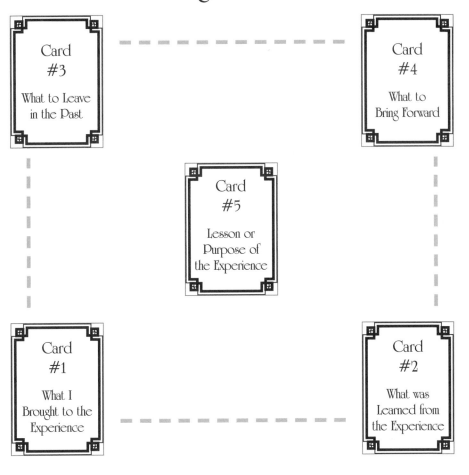

Card #3

What to Leave
in the Past

Card #4

What to
Bring Forward

Card #5

Lesson or
Purpose of
the Experience

Card #1

What I
Brought to the
Experience

Card #2

What was
Learned from
the Experience

As you begin to garner the overall sense of the reading, keep these thoughts in mind:

Is there a preponderance of any one element?

Do Major Arcana cards make a prominent statement?

Did the Fool, Emperor, or Death card in particular make an appearance?

Do any Personality cards appear and/or make a statement?

Which particular card(s) stand(s) out?

Do reversed cards appear? If so, what does the reversed position depict or imply?

Does tension exist between any of the cards within the spread?

Is there an easy flow between any of the cards within the spread?

Are there cards that prompt familiar thoughts or feelings?

Are there cards that bring in new thoughts or feelings to consider?

Do matters seem to be resolved?

Are the places where work may need to occur in order to accomplish closure?

Once the bird's eye view of the reading has been established, move into interpretation of the individual cards in their specific positions. Use these ideas to help gather information from each card within the spread:

Card #1
What attitudes, abilities, and issues were with me at the beginning of this experience?

How was I feeling at the beginning of this experience?

What was in my mind at the beginning of this experience?

How well did I know myself before this experience?

What was I wanting/needing at the beginning of this experience?

Who was I when this experience began?

Card #2
What changed during this experience?

How am I a different person than I was before this experience?

What new ideas have been integrated?

How have my feelings changed?

How am I strengthened and matured by this experience?

How does my life look differently as a result of this experience?

Card #3
What have I resolved as a result of this experience?

What is no longer part of my life as a result of this experience?

Which habits have been broken?

To what/whom am I no longer attached?

What old hurts or disappointments can be left behind as a result of this experience?

What no longer serves me?

Card #4
What are the gifts of this experience?

How has life been enhanced by this experience?

What has been integrated as part of this experience?

What from this experience will never leave me?

How does this experience provide strength and courage for the future?

How can I best honor the memory of this experience?

Card #5
How has this been a pivotal experience in my life?

Which transformational forces were parts of this experience?

How has this experience changed who I am?

Do I see the hand of Fate/Creator/Spirit in this experience?

How am I a better person for having had this experience?

What did I need to learn about life that this experience showed me?

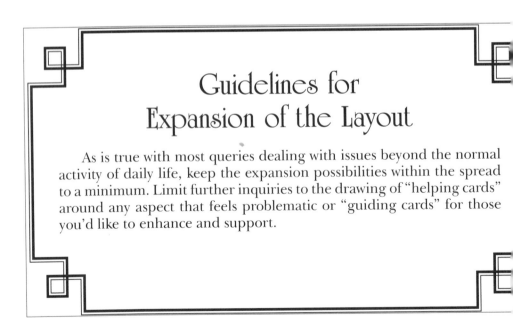

Guidelines for Expansion of the Layout

As is true with most queries dealing with issues beyond the normal activity of daily life, keep the expansion possibilities within the spread to a minimum. Limit further inquiries to the drawing of "helping cards" around any aspect that feels problematic or "guiding cards" for those you'd like to enhance and support.

Personal Development & Life's Big Questions
1- or 2-Card Draws

Ours is a time in history when many people actively participate in their process of personal growth and development. In other days and times, folks by necessity were more concerned with basic survival and the struggles of day-to-day living than with matters of psychological exploration and personal growth.

These days, thanks to science, technology, and numerous other sociological and cultural factors, "self-help" has become big business. We are surrounded by its relevant information in a manner unheard of in decades past. From Sigmund Freud to Carl Jung, from Joseph Campbell to Eckhart Tolle, the modern mindset is very much focused on self-awareness and the understanding of consciousness.

Aside from the cultural and technological components contributing to the self-help phenomenon, there is an historical aspect driving this movement toward introspection and consciousness-raising: an intrinsic motivation in and of recent generations to make a forward leap in our understanding of and participation in the world. Since the 1960s, the mantra has continued, sometimes as a quiet rumble and sometimes blaring in our ears, "It's time to change the world!" And please make note: If you have taken the time to learn the Tarot, you've become a participant in this forward leap of consciousness.

Think of it: Millions and millions of Tarot decks have been sold worldwide since the 1960s. These decks are not being bought by hoards of fledgling Tarot readers, but rather are purchased by everyday people. This in itself is quite a shift in the demographic of Tarot ownership, a sharp contrast to the limited ownership by the elite ruling families in the fifteenth and sixteenth centuries, or by the occultists and magicians working during Victorian times. Average, ordinary people now buy Tarot decks (millions and millions of Tarot decks!) and that in itself will ensure a steady movement toward the advancement of consciousness.

As we explore personal growth issues with the Tarot, the notion of this being an active process will be accentuated. There won't be a specific layout or spread for this area of query, although any of the layouts delineated herein can be used as a template for questions supporting personal development. Nor will any queries here begin with the words "when" or "will I." (Empowerment is an indispensable aspect of personal growth.)

You will find suggested lines of questioning listed below. You might use these queries and intentions at the beginning of each calendar year, on birthdays, or any time when recounting the past and assessing the future is relevant. Or it may be that the self-reflection intrinsic with these types of queries is a continuing work in progress, part of a regular practice of introspection and self-examination.

> **Important:** We must keep the queries in this realm open yet simplified because the active process of personal development is subjective.

We all swim solo in the process of burgeoning enlightenment. Although people around us may be supportive of and even integral to this process, we each walk a unique path toward a life with personal significance and meaning.

Questions regarding this part of life need to reflect and support the subjective tenor of the personal search for truth, yet like all queries, need to be concisely phrased and clearly intended. Speak from the heart; the Tarot can be a guide through some pretty challenging terrain. Here are some sample thoughts from which to take your own steps toward a deeper understanding of yourself. Draw only one or two cards for each question:

What particular strengths and abilities do I bring to life at the present time?

How can I develop or enhance these strengths and abilities?

What is at the root of my fears?

What can help me cope with my fears?

What can help me resolve my fears?

What lessons have I learned through recent experiences?

How can I best love and support myself?

How do I hold myself back?

What might be my next area of personal challenge?

What can I do in order to be satisfied, successful, and effective in my work life?

What can I do in order to be content in my physical body?

What can I do in order to be satisfied, successful, and effective in my family life?

What can I do in order to be satisfied, successful, and effective in my relationship life?

What can I do in order to be satisfied, successful, and effective in my creativity?

What can help me develop peace of mind?

How can I keep my thoughts from controlling my life?

How can I use my mind to create peace in my life?

What can I do in order to be satisfied, successful, and effective in my spiritual life?

What might enhance my connection to spirituality?

Are there blocks or hindrances to a connection with Spirit?

What is my life's greatest challenge?

What is my single greatest asset?

Yes, there are many, many ways to access help and guidance from the Tarot! As a polite host might say to a guest, "Don't be afraid to ask for what you need." As was stated earlier, if a matter is of importance to you, you can ask it of the Tarot.

This goes for the Big Questions as well as for the mundane matters of daily living. The rules for the Big Questions are going to be the same as they have been for all the other spreads and layouts within this book: Set a clear intention and phrase a concise query.

Here, as with personal growth questions, use a one- or two-card draw. Big Questions needn't be complicated by lots of cards. Use queries such as, but not limited to, the following themes:

What is my life's purpose?

What must I do to discover my purpose?

What would give more meaning to my life?

How can I best be of service in the world?

How can I find support for who I really am?

What is waiting to be brought into my life?

What does Spirit/Source want me to know?

What are my most useful gifts and abilities?

Who am I at my core?

What might be this life's biggest lesson for me?

What might be important for me to accomplish in this life?

What is it that I offer to other people?

What is it that I receive from my connections with other people?

Use these types of queries to support your authenticity, your self-awareness, and your self-respect.

> The world needs the best "you" you can be. Let the Tarot guide and support you in that unfolding process.

Conclusion

The adventure of learning the Tarot is a lot like the process of chopping firewood, in that it warms the participant twice over: once while wielding the ax to chop the wood and then again when the wood is burning in the fireplace.

The "chopping of the wood" of Tarot (the learning of card symbols and meanings, defining astrological and numerological significances, establishing connections to other metaphysical systems such as Kaballah and alchemy, etc.) is a task left to other resources. (A short list of essential Tarot resources can be found at the back of this book.)

This book is about the "warmth of the fire," the utilization of Tarot knowledge in ways that enhance life, foster personal growth, and expand consciousness. By using the spreads, layouts, methods, and ideas discussed herein, you will benefit from the glow of Tarot's fire, finding comfort through a deepened awareness of the inner nature of humanity and a greater understanding of those matters which touch us to the core.

Reader's Check List

This book has provided easy-to-use templates for particular lines of questioning. As the ongoing relationship with the Tarot develops, you will use these and many other formats as you seek clarity and guidance from the Tarot. Regardless of the method utilized, here's a reminder about the essential keys for getting the most from any Tarot layout:

- **First and foremost:** Acknowledge what intuition tells you. As has been reiterated, the importance of listening to and using one's intuition cannot be overstated.
- Set a clear intention for the reading. Before cards are selected, know what you're doing and why you're doing it.
- Once cards appear in the layout, take a few moments to recognize the overall tone or feeling of the cards as they first appear.

- Make note of the particular elements/suits which appear in the layout.
- Notice any recurring numbers, symbols, elements, and colors within the layout.
- If Personality cards appear, give thought to what the People are doing, to what/whom they may or may not be facing, how they're directing their energy, and in what context within the layout they appear.
- If you've chosen to consider the reversed position of cards as a relevant factor in your reading, make note of which cards are reversed and what that might imply.
- Delve into specific card meanings and interpretations once you're settled on the information gleaned from these overviews.

Remembering Relativity

The entire process of learning and reading Tarot is, from beginning to end, an ongoing exercise in relativity. This is what makes a Tarot reading the "mirror of the given moment." It is true that:

- The cards each have a field of meaning but no one card has only one single interpretation.
- The explicit meaning of any one card is ultimately determined by the reader's belief systems and world view.
- The interpretation of any one card is influenced by all the other cards which appear along with it.
- The interpretation of any one card is affected by the reader's – as well as the querent's – world views and belief systems.
- The interpretation of any one card is affected by the nature of the query for which it has been drawn.

"What does Card X mean?" It depends. "Does Card X always mean the same thing?" Not really. "What does it mean when Card X appears with Card Y?" It depends. "Does Card X mean the same thing to everyone?" Not necessarily. "When is Card X a positive thing and when is it negative thing?" It's often a little of both.

Honestly, how does one manage it? It is managed – and made effective – by establishing a solid base of Tarot knowledge, developing an intimate relationship with intuition, and maintaining a feel for the fluidity of the moment. This is the art of Tarot. This is what makes it so wonderfully alive and relevant to everyday living.

Final Thoughts

The Tarot is more than the mirror for any given moment. Tarot is alive and relevant in today's world because it is part of the shift in the personal and the collective consciousness. Tarot informs, clarifies, and supports efforts to increase the awareness of choices, actions, and responsibilities. It reminds us of our gifts, our blessings, our shortcomings, and our opportunities. It acknowledges our strengths, our value as a unique individual, and the movement of the soul as it makes its way along this worldly path.

Already inside of you is all that is needed to participate in this wondrous process. Firstly, you have the innate wisdom of intuition. Secondly, you spring from the essential web that intertwines all of reality, and therefore are automatically connected to everyone and everything. This is no longer a statement made confidently only in the minds of mystics, spiritualists, and philosophers; this is the quantum reality of the twenty-first century.

While the remarkable findings of quantum physics are turning traditional science on its ear, those same findings are validating truths which have been known to mystics, spiritualists, and philosophers since the dawn of recorded history. A quantum concept relevant to the Tarot process is the fundamental notion that at the deepest level of matter, behind the molecule, underneath the atom, and supporting the minutest subatomic particles, is a flowing ground of being, a place of pure possibilities and endless potential. This "unified field" of reality is the most basic net of potentialities from which all of reality springs. *All* of reality, including you and me…including the Tarot.

Since we are all a part of a single system of interrelated connections, it is not a stretch of the imagination to realize that all knowledge, events, and circumstance are present and available within the unified field. As Tarot readers, we are, essentially, intentionally and consciously "fishing" in the unified field for our answers. Intuition is the bait; the Tarot cards are the fishing pole; intention is the hook.

It is my hope that this book has ignited a spark of interest in the Tarot, that it will compel you to seek out the insight, wisdom, humor, and pleasure intrinsic to this system of symbols. May you find joy in the process of learning the Tarot and through that process, more fully understand yourself and others. And while on that journey, recognize that a multitude of cards does not equate with more accurate or better information, and that things don't have to be complex in order to be true.

Appendix

Quick & Easy Tarot Card Reference Guide

Here's an easy reference guide for the 78 cards of the Tarot system: a generalized overview of the cards and a short explanation of how each one fits into the overall scheme of interpretation.

Use this reference to help zero in on basic card meanings, while at the same time remembering that it is the intrinsic nature of each card to contain many different facets, attributes, qualities, and potential interpretations. Some cards are very precise in their meaning, while others have a broad field of interpretation with seemingly-contradictory implications. Also bear in mind that card significances are impacted by other cards within the layout, as well as by the posited query and the intention of the reading.

Major Arcana

The 22 cards of the MAJOR ARCANA are the expression of the transpersonal forces of growth and development. These are the archetypes of human existence, those universal energies which are beyond the scope of personal initiative and control.

The Fool

The source of all being; one's most authentic Self; non-rational confidence in all things; an *in the moment* experience of life without concern for the outcome.

The Magician

The expression of creative control in one's life; the capacity to invent and to take advantage of opportunities; knowledge of one's gifts and abilities; using one's initiative to create change.

The High Priestess

The essence of intuition; one's inner voice; the nebulous nature of unconscious knowledge; patience.

The Empress

The essence of "Mother;" the nurturer and facilitator; the forces in and of the natural world; collaboration.

The Emperor

The essence of "Father;" the builder and creator; the force of the intellect and reason; control.

The Hierophant

The teacher and mentor; guidance received from traditional resources; the structures of society, culture, and religion; the healer.

The Lovers

Choices made consciously and with intention; personal authenticity; balance in all aspects of one's life; harmonization of opposing energies.

The Chariot

The force of the personality in action; focused attention along a certain path; confidence; hubris.

Strength

Inner struggles; the difficult task of integrating new experience; challenges which promote new ways of being; an attempt to balance various aspects of life.

The Hermit

Self-reliance; inner wisdom; the path of self-knowledge; isolation.

The Wheel

The inevitability of change; endings followed by beginnings; the effects of destiny, karma, and fate; matters being impacted by timing.

Justice

Knowing what is true; the impartiality of the truth; fairness and objectivity; laws and morals.

The Hanged Man

The need for patience; suspension of willpower; standing on the sidelines while matters unfold; unwillingness to accept responsibility.

Death

Profound change; loss of self-identifying factors; the end of an era; a time of personal renewal.

Temperance

Patience; healing; awareness of divine timing in all matters; forgiveness.

The Devil

Displaced personal power; blame, shame, or guilt; illusions; addictions.

The Tower

Sudden change; radical shifts in perception; unexpected news or awareness; breaking free from outworn routines.

The Star

Hope and renewal; the harmonizing of one's spiritual and physical natures; creative imagining; a clean slate on which to build a new life.

The Moon

Indirect or diffuse awareness; an active dreamlike or psychic state; confrontation with the unknown; confusion and uncertainty.

The Sun

Joyful self-expression; playful pleasures; boundless enthusiasm; a birth or a death.

Judgment

Crossroads; time for irrevocable decisions; "hearing the call;" the culmination of knowledge leading to action.

The World

Completion of a cycle; resolution; attainment; the successful integration of disparate elements thereby creating a totality of experience.

Minor Arcana

The 56 cards within the MINOR ARCANA address the particulars of human experience by describing what we do, how we feel, what is happening, what we think, and how we manage our worldly reality. The ACE card through the TEN card of each suit show specific experiences within that suit; the COURT Cards express the ways in which an individual deals with or manages those experiences. (The COURT Cards also can represent actual people relevant to the query.) Each suit within the MINOR ARCANA is ruled by one of the four elements of existence: fire, water, air and earth.

SUIT OF WANDS

Ruled by the element of fire, the suit of WANDS expresses the forces of inspiration, creativity, drive and focus, self-expression, willpower, competitiveness, determination, ego strength, and the inspirational aspects of spirituality.

Ace of Wands

Initiative; boundless energy; creative inspiration; personal power.

Two of Wands

Envisioning the future; readiness for change; creative imagining; goal-setting.

Three of Wands

Embarking on new adventures; walking through doors of opportunity; preparations having been completed; journey or travel.

Four of Wands

Celebration; harmony in the home; enjoyment at work or play; esthetic pleasures.

Five of Wands

Lack of focus; activity without progress; differing wants and needs expressing themselves within oneself or a group; being required to "wear many hats."

Six of Wands

Success; reward for one's efforts; support of community; pride in one's accomplishments.

Seven of Wands

Inner and/or outer battles; meeting a challenge head on; creating problems where they don't exist; taking a stand or defending a position.

Eight of Wands

Ease; fast pace of activity; various forces aligning themselves toward a common goal; matters moving quickly toward resolution.

Nine of Wands

Perseverance; strength in the midst of struggle; weariness; battles having been won but the war yet to win.

Ten of Wands

Endings; permission to lay down the load; frustration; release from struggle.

Page of Wands

The Instigator; curiosity; restlessness; a creative spark.

Knight of Wands

The Adventurer; willingness to take risks; youthful enthusiasm and unbridled passions; this Knight goes on a quest in search of challenge and excitement.

Queen of Wands

The Heroine; a motivated and dynamic person; an effective manager and multi-tasker; selfishness.

King of Wands

The Leader; a forceful personality; a visionary; willful and potentially reckless.

Suit of Cups

Rules by the element of water, the suit of Cups encompasses the realm of relationships, one's sense of community and connections with others, compassion, empathy, nurturance, the dream life, psychic ability, and the aspects of spirituality which open the heart to unconditional acceptance and love.

Ace of Cups

Self-acceptance; spiritual guidance; gratitude and compassion; fertility.

Two of Cups

Emotional balance; new relationship; attraction; separate but equal components working together harmoniously.

Three of Cups

Support of friends; a rich and varied social life; successful partnerships; celebration.

Four of Cups

Self-doubt; emotional uncertainty; resistance to change; inability to make a decision.

Five of Cups

Loss; disappointment; betrayal; the need to mourn.

Six of Cups

Friendship; sisterhood/brotherhood; mutual enjoyment in partnerships; ease in relationship.

Seven of Cups

Self-doubt; emotional confusion; projection; the search for inner wisdom.

Eight of Cups

Change in relationship; the wisdom to leave behind what is outworn; emotional detachment; self-empowerment resulting from emotional difficulty.

Nine of Cups

Satisfaction; contentment; selfishness; emotional needs being fulfilled.

Ten of Cups

A marriage of the hearts; happy home and family; wishes granted; the responsibilities of family life.

Page of Cups

The Sensitive Child: vulnerability; the stirrings of self-awareness; introspection.

Knight of Cups

The Dreamer; a gentle person with an easy-going nature; one who is soft-spoken and sincere; this Knight goes on the quest in whatever direction his heart and soul demands.

Queen of Cups

The Feeler; emotional intensity; psychic and intuitive abilities; jealousy.

King of Cups

The Controller; strong nurturing force; thrives on relationships yet can be tangled in/by them; resists changes in the emotional status quo.

Suit of Swords

Ruled by the element of air, the suit of Swords expresses the world of thinking, perceptions, ideals, and principles, one's sense of truth and justice, laws, moral codes, new ideas, world views, mental constructs, and the epiphanic aspects of spirituality.

Ace of Swords

Absolute knowing; clear thinking; the awareness of truth; assertion.

Two of Swords

A quiet mind; inner focus; the denial of what is obvious; patience.

Three of Swords

Disappointment; shattered illusions; the potential to heal an old hurt; the need to reassess a situation.

Four of Swords

Resting in what is true; a time of recuperation; finding peace in the midst of turmoil; deciding not to decide.

Five of Swords

Boundaries being drawn; taking an unpopular stand; meeting aggression with defense rather than offense; self-protection through stubborn assertion.

Six of Swords

Release of stress; a physical move or travel; the need to evolve beyond something or someone; postponement of a decision.

Seven of Swords

Conflict avoidance; secret-keeping; tact; deceit.

Eight of Swords

Mental blocks; indecision; fear of change; problems having been created by self-limiting thoughts and beliefs.

Nine of Swords

Overwhelming anxiety; taking on more than one can handle; unrealistic sense of doom and responsibility; sleeplessness and worry.

Ten of Swords

Finality; foregone conclusions having been realized; resignation; release from stress.

Page of Swords

The Rabble Rouser; brainstorming; wit and insight; one who engages in thoughtless gossip.

Knight of Swords

The Communicator; someone interesting in the learning of and the expression of differing viewpoints; creative intelligence; this Knight goes on his quest in the exploration of thoughts and ideas.

Queen of Swords

The Advocate; a person of high principles and non-negotiable opinions; intelligence in service of a cause; emotionally remote.

King of Swords

The Enforcer; one who upholds laws and values; a leader and decision-maker; unyielding and unsympathetic.

Suit of Pentacles

Ruled by the element of earth, the suit of PEN-TACLES reflects physical solidity and security, money matters, work issues, health and body issues, stability and groundedness, one's sense of personal safety, all practical concerns, and the "doing good works" aspect of spirituality.

Ace of Pentacles

New financial opportunities; an change related to work or home; a renewed sense of security and stability; generous support or assistance from others.

Two of Pentacles

Transition; travel; uncertainty without instability; the presence of options.

Three of Pentacles

Firm foundation; a healthy body; a secure position from which to move forward; effective working partnerships.

Four of Pentacles

Resistance to change; maintaining one's position; playing it "close to the vest;" self-preservation.

Five of Pentacles

Expectations of failure; depravation mentality; lack of spiritual connection; potential loss of income.

Six of Pentacles

Shared resources and responsibilities; available help in times of need; a mutually beneficial arrangement; a "give-and-take" situation.

Seven of Pentacles

The availability of options; taking time to consider choices carefully; reevaluation of past efforts; lack of motivation.

Eight of Pentacles

Rearrangement of assets; taking a new approach to a situation; pride in one's effort and workmanship; a shift in the status of home or career.

Nine of Pentacles

Confidence in one's abilities; appreciation for the "good things in life;" pride in accomplishments; a self-reliant person.

Ten of Pentacles

Family and cultural traditions; the institution of marriage; a solid and secure situation which is unlikely to change; wealth and success.

Page of Pentacles

The Apprentice; someone with a plan for the future; undertaking the long-term task of building of a home or business; experiencing life from a new perspective.

Knight of Pentacles

The Worker; a stable and reliable person; one who is adept in mechanics or handicrafts; this Knight remains on his quest until his project has been completed.

Queen of Pentacles

The Nurturer; the ideal of constancy and comfort; the traditional wife and mother; one who is self-employed.

King of Pentacles

The Business Person; one who upholds traditional means and values; someone who can stubbornly resist change; a person who understands the workings of the world.

List of Resources

Introductory Material

Arrien, Angeles. *The Tarot Handbook*. New York, NY: Tarcher/Putnam, 1997.(Tarot symbols from a psychological, mythological, and cross-cultural perspective, illustrated with Aleister Crowley's *Thoth Tarot* deck.)

Fairfield, Gail. *Every Day Tarot: A Choice Centered Book*. York Beach Maine: Weiser Books, 2002. (An accessible guide for using the Tarot as a tool for personal empowerment and self discovery.)

Greer, Mary K. *Tarot For Your Self: A Workbook for Personal Transformation*. Franklin Lakes, NJ: New Page Books, 2002. (All you ever need to know about the basics of Tarot and then some. Thorough and eminently usable, a must-have for any Tarot library.)

Intermediate Material

Fiorini, Jeanne. *Invitation to Wonder: Real Life Insights Through the Tarot*, Portland, Maine: Suite One Publishing, 2002. (A review of actual Tarot readings in a narrative style. Informative, inspiring, easy to read for the novice and a joyful affirmation for the more experienced practitioner.)

Nichols, Sallie. *Jung and Tarot: An Archetypal Journey*. York Beach Maine: Samuel Weiser Inc., 1980. (An excellent and thorough review of the Major Arcana from the viewpoint of Jungian psychology.)

Pollack, Rachel. *The Forest of Souls: A Walk Through the Tarot*. Woodbury MN: Llewellyn Publications, 2002. (A poetic and imaginative exploration of card methods, lines of questioning, and interpretation as only Rachel Pollack can deliver.)

Quantum Physics & Psychic Phenomena

Radin, Dean. *The Conscious Universe: The Scientific Truth of Psychic Phenomena*. New York, NY: HarperEdge, 1997. (The scientific backbone for the validation of paranormal and psychic phenomena, from a senior scientist at the Institute of Noetic Sciences.)

Talbot, Michael. *The Holographic Universe*. New York, NY: HarperCollins, 1991. (A groundbreaking book bringing the mind-bending theories of quantum physics to the general public. A readable and inspiring overview of the marriage between science and mysticism.)

Movie CD Boxed Set

What the Bleep: Down the Rabbit Hole/Quantum Edition. Captured Light Industries and Lord of the Wind Films LLC, 2004. (Original theatrical version of the movie *What the Bleep Do We Know*, additional interviews, extended director's cut of the film, and filmmakers' Q & A. A great combination of storyline, physics, spirituality, and shattering new concepts about how the universe really works. Also visit www. whatthebleep.com for more information.)